THE ULTIMATE GUIDE TO STEPPING
INTO CONTROL OF YOUR OWN LIFE

Get it Together Forever!

SIMPLE STRATEGIES FOR DEALING WITH STRESS, ANXIETY AND ALL THAT LIFE THROWS AT YOU

Dr Tracey Zielinski

First published by Ultimate World Publishing 2021
Copyright © 2021 Tracey Zielinski

ISBN

Paperback: 978-1-922714-11-4
Ebook: 978-1-922714-12-1

Tracey Zielinski has asserted her rights under the Copyright, Designs and Patents Act 1988 to be identified as the author of this work. The information in this book is based on the author's experiences and opinions. The publisher specifically disclaims responsibility for any adverse consequences which may result from use of the information contained herein. Permission to use information has been sought by the author. Any breaches will be rectified in further editions of the book.

All rights reserved. No part of this publication may be reproduced, stored in or introduced into a retrieval system, or transmitted in any form, or by any means (electronic, mechanical, photocopying, recording or otherwise) without the prior written permission of the author. Any person who does any unauthorised act in relation to this publication may be liable to criminal prosecution and civil claims for damages. Enquiries should be made through the publisher.

Cover design: Ultimate World Publishing
Layout and typesetting: Ultimate World Publishing
Editor: James Salmon
Cover photo by: Dr Tracey Zielinski, taken while walking 'The Path of the Gods' on the Amalfi Coast, Italy, on 9 May 2017.

Ultimate World Publishing
Diamond Creek,
Victoria Australia 3089
www.writeabook.com.au

What People are Saying...

Get it Together Forever is a book with the capacity to help a lot of people. Tracey has an innate ability to explain complex ideas in simple terms, and the strategies that she has outlined throughout the book are both easy to implement and extremely effective. Be it for those struggling with a particular aspect of life, individuals looking to complement pre-existing coping mechanisms or someone else entirely, *Get it Together Forever* is an invaluable support tool.

James Salmon
Editor, Writer

Get it Together Forever is a refreshing, unique and confidence-inspiring read. The clear explanations of the strategies in this book are easy to both understand and put into action in everyday life. The more I consciously practised utilising the new strategies the easier they became. I changed; and the world around me became much brighter, calmer, and no longer overwhelming. By choosing to adopt the strategies in this book, *Get it Together Forever*, I am confident that, like me, you too can change your life forever. I applaud Tracey for sharing her wisdom in the writing of this book.

Robyn Worthy
Community Support Worker

Utilising over 20 years of specialised knowledge and experience within the field of clinical psychology, Dr Tracey Zielinski skilfully synthesises evidence-based literature in mental health and integrates key concepts with practical and effective management strategies embedded in established cognitive behavioural therapy and mindfulness frameworks. *Get it Together Forever* will help you gain a greater understanding of yourself and empower you to cope with various challenges that life may throw at you. A scintillating read!

Dr Mia Mariani
Clinical Psychologist

Dedication

To my husband, Terry, whose support and feedback have been invaluable on this journey. Thank you for your honesty in reviewing my work. *Get it Together Forever* is a better book because of your input. I will forever be grateful for the encouragement you have given me to follow my passion.

To my mother and stepfather who have always believed in me and encouraged me. You inspire me with all you do and all you are. You have taught me that it is never too late to follow my dreams.

Disclaimer

All information provided in *Get it Together Forever* is general in nature and is provided for information purposes only. The information contained within this book should not be used to diagnose or treat psychological or psychiatric conditions, nor should it be used as an alternative to obtaining professional therapeutic advice from a qualified psychologist, psychiatrist, or medical practitioner.

Contents

What People are Saying . . .	iii
Dedication	v
Disclaimer	vii
Introduction	1
SECTION ONE: Setting the Scene	**7**
Chapter One: Behind the Scenes	9
Chapter Two: Learning to Chill	17
Chapter Three: How Long is a Ball of String?	31
Chapter Four: Talk Yourself Up	43
SECTION TWO: Getting to Know Yourself Better	**65**
Chapter Five: The Power of Two! The Power of You!	67
Chapter Six: Get it Together Forever	83
SECTION THREE: You Want More?	**93**
Chapter Seven: What If?	97
Chapter Eight: Too Many Boxes!	119
Chapter Nine: The Swamp Monster	143
Chapter Ten: Breaking the Big Bad Wolf of Habits	165
About the Author	189
Acknowledgements	191

Introduction

As I write this book, the world is in the midst of a global pandemic. Life as we knew it has changed. In some ways, it has likely changed forever. We are all aware of the devastation the COVID-pandemic has created, the impact it has had on so many lives.

As a psychologist, I along with my colleagues have seen an escalation in the demand for mental health services. Many psychologists have had their waitlists blow out to months rather than weeks. The demand for crisis counselling services is higher than it has ever been.

The pandemic has inspired people who have never before sought psychological assistance to reach out for help. Where once there was a stigma attached to seeking psychological support, a growing number of people are recognising that seeking support is simply common-sense when they are struggling with the stuff life throws at them.

Many people I have seen in private practice do not have significant mental health issues. They are simply struggling in the moment. Many of these people do not require intensive and lengthy therapeutic assistance. Often with psychoeducation and introduction to a range of simple, effective strategies, they can step back into feeling in control of their lives.

It is with these people in mind that I have written *Get it Together Forever*.

It is my hope that ultimately this book can help reduce psychologists' waiting lists. It is my hope that in reducing waiting lists, psychologists can give the support and attention needed to those people who need regular and intensive psychological therapy without burning themselves out in the process.

Get it Together Forever is not meant to replace therapy. It is, however, an incredibly useful tool to allow those people who are ready and able to become more resilient to do so.

The process I have developed and outlined in the first two sections of this book has its roots in cognitive behaviour therapy (CBT) and mindfulness.

There are three sections to the book. Each section should be read, and the information and strategies practised, before the next section is read. Subsequent sections build on the information and strategies given in previous sections.

The book is meant to be read and actioned in the following manner:

Introduction

1. Read Section One, practising the strategies as you go.
2. Practise the tools and strategies taught in the first section for at least one week before moving on.
3. Read Section Two, practising the strategies as you go.
4. Practise the tools and strategies taught in the first and second sections for at least one further week before moving on.
5. If you feel that you would benefit from more information and strategies to complete your transformation, then go to Section Three. Select and read the chapters that apply to you.

With consistent practice, you should notice a positive shift in your ability to take control of your own actions and reactions within the first week of reading Section One.

Section One

Section One concentrates on helping you step away from reactive behaviours and habits that simply are not helpful to you. I build a simple-to-understand model of brain function as it applies to reactive and proactive behaviours. I talk about the body and consider how it functions when you are distressed and when you are relaxed. I then show you a simple and effective method to shift from feeling distressed to feeling relaxed. I give you a simple model for shifting habits that are not working for you. Finally, I uncover the mysteries of how you sabotage yourself with your thoughts, and most importantly, what you can do instead.

Section Two

Section Two is designed to be read after you have practised the information in Section One for at least one week. It focuses on building a good relationship with yourself, which in turn has a positive impact on your relationships and interactions with others. Section Two concludes with a review of all the information covered in the first two sections. These two sections together outline my common-sense process. For many people, the information contained just within these two sections will be enough for them to step away from their unhelpful behavioural patterns, build resilience, and transform their lives.

Section Three

Section Three contains additional useful information covering a range of common issues many people present with when seeking professional assistance. It may be that it can provide the last piece of the puzzle to help you step away from old unhelpful patterns.

Chapter Seven focuses on anxiety.
Chapter Eight focuses on stress.
Chapter Nine focuses on depression.
Chapter Ten focuses on habits that seem resistant to change.

The information and strategies embedded within this book will help many people step into control of their own actions and reactions and get it together forever.

Introduction

Other people may find the information in this book to be a useful adjunct to therapy with a qualified professional.

I want to reiterate, however, that *Get it Together Forever* is not designed to be a replacement for therapy. If you have significant levels of psychological or psychiatric distress then seek professional help.

SECTION ONE

Setting the Scene

Section One gives you the framework you will use as you begin to build a set of new, helpful habits. This section provides a simple overview of the brain and body and lets you in on the secret of taking control of your actions and reactions moving forward. Stepping away from self-sabotage is much easier when you understand how to dismantle the roadblocks you have been constructing. Knowledge is power. Use it well.

CHAPTER ONE

Behind the Scenes

Ever been on an emotional roller coaster? Put your foot in your mouth, and only taken it out to replace it with the other foot? Snapped at someone after a stressful day at work? Felt scared even though you knew there was nothing to fear? Let your frustration bubble to the surface? Been told you have anger management issues? Have you ever told yourself, "I'm not going to react like that again", only to find yourself reacting in exactly the same way the next time something similar happens? I know I have!

Each and every one of us has times where we lose control of our own emotional response. At these times, we react automatically to whatever situation we are facing. When we react automatically we are falling back on habit or learned behaviour.

The question is how do you stop being reactive and start being proactive? How do you go about deliberately choosing your behavioural response to get the best result possible? And why is it so hard to change your emotional habits?

The truth is, it's not difficult to change a habit, a pattern of behaviour, but it does take effort. It also helps to know how to go about it.

I'm going to share with you some simple ideas and strategies to help you create habits that you deliberately choose because you feel they will work better than your old habits.

Let's start by creating a framework to build on. In this case, it's important to have some knowledge of the roles of two very different areas of the brain.

Thinking Brain

Our thinking brain is the clever bit. It keeps growing and developing until we reach our mid-twenties. It takes in and processes information from all our senses and from different centres of our brains. It brings various bits of information together to make sense of them. It does all our planning and problem-solving. It's the part of our brain that puts us significantly above animals in the intelligence stakes. It can be logical, sensible and scientific. It is not emotional. It's the thinking centre of our brain.

If you rest your left forehead in the palm of your left hand, the thinking brain is located in there, tucked into your hand.

Behind the Scenes

The technical name for this area, which you don't need to know but may be interested in knowing, is the dorsolateral prefrontal cortex (DLPFC for short). Personally, I call it the thinking brain or the adult area of the brain.

I call it the adult area because it develops until you are in your mid-twenties and it's clever and rational.

This area allows you to take manual control of your actions, behaviours, and reactions. It allows you to plan and problem-solve issues as they arise. It allows you to work out the best strategy to deal with a particular problem, person or situation.

So, why don't you allow your thinking brain to take charge more often? Why is it so often not in evidence when you step into emotionally reactive mode?

The one problem with the thinking brain is that it's actually quite slow to get started. In order for your thinking brain to make a decision about how to respond in a situation, it must take in and integrate all the relevant information. While this doesn't necessarily take long, it does take a noticeable amount of time.

This brings us to the second area of the brain that plays a rather important role in maintaining your emotional habits and reactive behaviours. Let me introduce you to the reactive loop.

Reactive Loop

Using your right hand, place your right thumb just to the right of the crown of your head. Put your right forefingers at the top of your forehead, just right of the centre. Now consider the area of brain that falls underneath your hand. This area is the home of your reactive loop. The loop includes part of the emotional centre of the brain, also known as the limbic system.

Compared with your thinking brain, this reactive loop is quite primitive. The most advanced bit of brain involved in this loop was fully formed when you were still very young. Because it involves the emotional centres of your brain, the behaviour driven by this loop tends to be reactive and emotion-based. What does that mean? It means that this is the loop that fires up when you are stressed, anxious, annoyed, angry, frustrated, etc.

The reactive loop is not under your manual control. The behaviours triggered by the reactive loop are often programmed in at quite a young age and tend not to be rational but rather emotional. It could quite reasonably be said that these irrational, emotion-based reactions rather resemble behaviours that we might expect to see from a young child who has not yet learned to consider another point of view – a child of perhaps around three years of age?

So why on Earth would you choose to let yourself launch into reactive mode when your thinking brain is likely to come up with a much more appropriate response in so many situations? Well, one of the problems is that the reactive loop is super quick to turn on. It literally flies into action in a fraction of a second. Reaction requires no thought. It is simply the triggering of a pre-programmed set of actions. By the time your thinking brain wakes up, you are likely to be in full flight, tearing downhill and picking up pace as you go.

In the next chapter, I will explore a simple, effective method you can use to stop that madcap gallop. For now, it's time to recap and create the first analogy that will help you take control and engage your thinking brain.

Adult Versus Three-Year-Old

Think about the difference in the way an adult and a three-year-old might react to something going bump in the night. The three-year-old may well hide under the sheets almost afraid to breathe in case the monster under the bed comes for them. The adult may be startled but will then switch on the light to see what made the noise. The first is an irrational, emotional response while the other is a thoughtful, logical response.

When you are angry, grumpy, frustrated, stressed, impulsive, snappy, irritable or scared, and you allow your behaviour to reflect these feelings, you run the serious risk of acting like a three-year-old. This reactive behaviour is automatic, emotional, and not designed to get the best result in virtually any situation.

You will get the best result in most situations when you turn to your thinking brain, your adult brain, for an action plan.

The reason I'm stressing the difference between adult versus three-year-old behaviour is simply that I think this sets up a beautiful analogy that lends itself perfectly to visualisation (the art of imagining).

Imagine This
Form a picture in your mind of yourself as a cool, calm, collected adult – logical, thoughtful, and in control of your own actions and reactions. Imagine the best version of yourself that you can. This image represents your adult brain – the part of you that allows you to confidently take control in any situation.

Now form a picture in your mind of yourself as the ugliest, brattiest three-year-old you can imagine – snotty nose, red-faced from screaming. This image represents your reactive loop – the part that controls your automatic, overly emotional reaction to situations.

Every time you catch yourself reacting like a three-year-old, bring up that image of you as a screaming brat. I can almost see the smile on your face now as you picture your snotty-nosed three-year-old in full flight. Imagine how much easier it will be to step away from that reactive behaviour now you have that image in your mind.

IN SUMMARY

Choose the adult over the three-year-old each time you catch yourself starting to become reactive and your behaviour will quickly start to be more considered and more likely to get you the results you want.

While you are learning to recognise your own three-year-old, be on the look-out for other people's three-year-olds. We all have an inner three-year-old. When you notice other people acting in three-year-old mode, you can choose to be the adult in the room. Think about the difference that might make to you and to the outcome of the situation you're in.

CHAPTER TWO

Learning to Chill

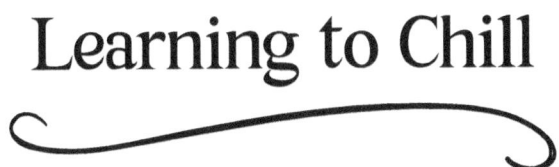

So, the big question is how do you learn to pull back from acting like a three-year-old and step into adult mode? When you are in the midst of emotionally reactive behaviours – snapping at your children, angry outbursts when something goes wrong, anxiety in a job interview, and so on – how do you stop?

The answer is surprisingly simple, but before I reveal the surprise, I want to spend a little more time setting the scene. They say that knowledge is power, and that makes sense to me. I believe that you are more likely to use the tools I'm giving you if you understand how and why they work.

The Unconscious System Rules!

In Chapter One, I spoke about the reactive loop which I likened to a bratty three-year-old. The reactive loop is part of a larger system we can think of as the unconscious system. The unconscious system, which some people call the lizard brain, runs all your bodily functions. It keeps your heart beating and the blood flowing through your body. It operates your digestive system and your sweat glands.

The unconscious system is also in charge of every movement you make and the production of every word you utter.

Try using your thinking brain to move your hand. Think hard at your hand, try to move it with your conscious mind . . . it doesn't work, does it?

Now just move your hand . . . easy, isn't it? Your unconscious system rules your body.

Your thinking brain, your adult brain, is not in charge of the actual physical act of movement any more than it controls an angry outburst. Your adult brain may well decide what to do, but it is your unconscious system that makes it physically happen.

A useful metaphor might be driving a car. You as the driver steer the car and decide how fast to go, but the actual mechanical system of the car allows it to move, change direction, and change speed.

Learning to Chill

Physical Reaction to an Emotional Reaction

Because the reactive loop is part of the unconscious system, you, as a human being, will always have a physical response when you experience an emotional response. This will be particularly noticeable when it is a strong emotional response. Whether the emotion is one you think of as negative or positive is irrelevant. When you feel depressed, your body experiences a heaviness, a sinking into the gut, your shoulders slump and you tend to feel exhausted. When you feel anxious, your heart rate increases, your palms may become sweaty, and your breathing tends to become faster and more shallow. Indeed, sometimes when you feel anxious, it may feel as though you are struggling to breathe at all. When you are happy, you smile, your body feels lighter and you tend to stand or sit up straighter.

Your emotions always come with a physical response. Possibly one of the best-known physical responses is associated with the fight or flight reflex.

Fight or Flight Reflex

The fight or flight reflex is triggered when you feel threatened in some way. In the best-case scenario, the fight or flight reflex is a useful and adaptive response to danger.

Think of primitive man, the first humans. Their world was one of extremes and dangers. They were hunter/gatherers competing for food and resources with other fierce predators. Imagine the men out hunting and a sabre-tooth tiger has his eyes on the same prey.

Imagine the sabre-tooth tiger looking at the men and thinking they look soft, slow and delicious. How did humans reach the top of the evolutionary tree without fangs and claws and bulky muscles?

The answer partly lies with the fight or flight reflex. In the presence of danger, or even the possible presence of danger, the fight or flight reflex kicks in. It triggers a physical response within the body:

- your heart pumps faster
- your breathing is faster and more shallow (hyperventilation) to bring in more oxygen
- adrenalin courses through your body
- the blood flow to the muscles focuses on pumping up the big muscles in your legs and arms, making you stronger and faster in order to fight or to run away.

This reflex is still in evidence today. We've all heard stories of a mother who has managed to lift a car to save her screaming child pinned underneath. These stories are not entirely urban legends. There are real-life examples of what appears to be superhuman strength in extreme circumstances when someone's life is at risk. A quick search of the internet found a couple of relevant examples including:

- Cecil Adams' story in 'The Straight Dope' (20 January 2006) about American, Angela Cavallo, who in 1982, while in her late fifties, raised a 1964 Chevy Impala which was pinning her teenage son after the jack had slipped while he was working underneath the car.

- Jon Haworth's story for ABC news (21 May 2021) showed video of Deputy Jon Holt from Virginia, America, single-handedly lifting a vehicle from a woman to allow her to free herself after a traffic accident.

The fight or flight reflex can give an incredible boost to your strength in times of extreme need. Your ancestors used the reflex to survive predators that were larger and stronger. Modern humans use it to rescue themselves or others in times of great need. It is undoubtedly useful when danger exists.

So where does the fight or flight reflex fit in your larger unconscious system? The fight or flight reflex is generally associated with what is known as the sympathetic nervous system, which is one part of the autonomic nervous system.

Autonomic Nervous System

The autonomic nervous system is in charge of running the body. It is the part of the unconscious system that keeps every aspect of the body functioning. The autonomic nervous system is generally broken into two distinct parts – the sympathetic nervous system and the parasympathetic nervous system.

Sympathetic Nervous System
Think of a big on/off switch. When the switch is turned on, the sympathetic nervous system primes you for action. When you are under stress or primed for danger, it is the sympathetic nervous system that is in play. The fight or

flight reflex is associated with the sympathetic nervous system. Stress also triggers the sympathetic nervous system. Functionally when your sympathetic nervous system is switched on you are in distress mode.

There is no doubt that if you are in physical and immediate danger, the triggering of the fight or flight reflex is going to give you your best chance of getting out of the situation alive. In this case, the fight or flight reflex is incredibly useful and adaptive. But what happens when your fight or flight reflex is triggered by something you think of as threatening that does not actually pose a clear and immediate physical danger? Well, this can lead to the birth of anxiety.

Anxiety. Anxiety can be thought of as a human reaction to an imagined danger. It might be triggered by a fear of public speaking, a fear of embarrassing yourself, worrying about "what if?", a medical condition that affects your breathing or your heart, or a thousand other situations.

It is important to realise that if there is a real physical danger then you are not experiencing anxiety. Rather, you are having a normal fight or flight reaction to a dangerous situation.

I think the most important aspect of anxiety is simply the fact that you do not feel in control. You do not feel in control of the situation. You do not feel in control of your own reaction to the situation.

A lot of people talk about anxiety as a response to not feeling safe, and there is no doubt that this comes into play, but personally I think the issue of control is more important. If you feel in control of your own actions and reactions then you tend to feel relatively safe. If you feel safe, however, it does not always suggest a sense of being in control.

Anxiety generally involves:

- negative self-talk
- a physical reaction to feeling out of control and/or unsafe (fight or flight reflex)
- behavioural avoidance of the situation.

Anxiety about a situation tends to build up over time and you become more and more likely to avoid the situation, which of course just makes the anxiety worse.

I will discuss anxiety in much more detail in Chapter Seven for those of you who struggle with these feelings.

Stress. Stress is a human response to feeling overwhelmed and over-burdened. The physical response to stress can include shallow breathing, increased heart rate, high blood pressure, muscular tension particularly in the shoulders and neck, stress headaches, reduced immune system response, and digestive issues such as reflux. In the worst-case scenario, high levels of chronic stress can lead to a stroke or heart attack.

Stress is your response to outside pressures, but you may well be guilty of adding your own burdens to the pile. High levels of stress often lead you to act out in ways that may involve snappiness, angry outbursts, impatience, intolerance, and impulsivity.

I will discuss stress in much more detail in Chapter Eight for those of you who are feeling overwhelmed by the pressures of life.

Parasympathetic Nervous System
When the switch linked to the autonomic nervous system is turned off, the parasympathetic nervous system is triggered. The parasympathetic nervous system places your body into a mode I refer to as relax mode. Ideally, unless you need to be primed for action your body is designed to function most effectively in relax mode.

Think about your digestive system, for example. There has been a lot of interest in recent years in the impact of stress and anxiety on the gut and its functioning. It is now widely understood that eating while you are stressed or anxious is likely to exacerbate issues such as reflux and indigestion. Think about it. Think back to your last bout of reflux or indigestion and consider your stress levels at the time. I can imagine you nodding as you make the connection. Fundamentally, what I'm saying here is if your body is in distress mode when you are eating your digestive system will not work properly.

It is not only your digestive system that works better when you are relaxed. Your blood pressure is better, your muscles are looser, you are more likely to be using your thinking brain, and so on. You function better when you are not in distress mode. Thus, when you are in a safe place with no danger threatening, ideally allow your body to slip into relax mode.

Learning to Chill

Shifting out of Distress Mode

So, the story so far . . . when you are distressed and responding to negative emotions, you tend to react like a bratty three-year-old. Often this response is a reaction to stress or anxiety, but regardless, it is a super quick reaction that is automatic rather than planned. Distress mode has a range of physical responses that are different from your physical responses when you are in relax mode.

In distress mode, your heart rate tends to be faster, your blood pressure higher, and your breathing relatively fast and shallow.

In relax mode, your heart rate is slower, your blood pressure is more likely to be in the normal range, and your breathing is deeper and slower.

So how do you step out of distress mode? Well, that's easier than you might think. I have up until now emphasised that the autonomic nervous system is outside our manual control, and that is indeed, for the most part, true. There is, however, one aspect of your physical functioning that you can manually control when you choose to, and that is your breathing.

You can choose to control your breath in a way that you cannot control your heart rate or your blood pressure or your digestive processes, and so on. And in controlling your breath, you can actually trigger a shift from distress mode to relax mode.

There are quite a few different ways that people teach breathing techniques. Some people teach a traditional diaphragmatic breathing technique. Some people refer to belly breathing. Singers are taught to control their breath and breathe into their diaphragm, for example. Yoga teaches its own breathing exercise. Some psychologists will teach you to focus on slow breaths for a particular number of seconds, holding your breath for a few seconds in between the in-breath and out-breath. Some will teach you to make your out-breath longer than your in-breath. Each of these techniques is beneficial if you use them properly.

Breathing is essential in every aspect of your life. It is an integral part of meditation, mindfulness exercises, yoga, Pilates, tai chi, qi gong, other martial arts, singing, sports, and more. One could say that controlling your breath is the first step towards controlling your life.

Breathe Through Your Eyes

My technique of breathing through the eyes is based on a simple diaphragmatic breathing exercise that I teach with a different focus. For many years I taught clients how to breathe into their diaphragm the old-fashioned way. It generally took them weeks to master the technique and some never did.

Now, rather than focusing on where the breath finishes, I encourage you to focus on where the breath begins. You will be breathing in through your nose and ideally out through your mouth, although if you are more comfortable breathing out through your nose, please do so. I generally find that most people master this technique in a breath or two.

The goal is for this to be as user-friendly for you as it can possibly be. After all, I want you to be comfortable doing this exercise, because personally I think it is one of the most effective tools in existence to help you relax and focus. I invariably say that if I could run around the entire world teaching every single person just one thing, this breathe through your eyes exercise would be it.

Instructions
Firstly, take a normal breath in through your nose. I want you to notice that the breath appears to flow into your nostrils and then simply disappear.

Now take another long slow breath in through your nose. This time I want you to imagine the breath flowing so far up your nose that it dives out through the bridge of your nose and flows into your eyes. Focus on feeling the breath in your eyes.

Some people describe feeling a sense of coolness or a light breeze across the surface of their eyes. Some people describe feeling as though their eyes are gently being sucked into their head a little. Personally, I feel my eyes being sucked into my head. It's a weird feeling, but the best thing is that my body immediately relaxes as the shift into relax mode is triggered.

Take the time now to practise the technique until you feel confident you've got it. Notice your body relax as you breathe. Notice your shoulders let go. Now, how easy was that?

Practice Makes Perfect
I suggest that you practise this technique at least five times a day, just for a few breaths unless you choose to do more. Ideally practise when you are relatively relaxed anyway, and then feel free to use the technique whenever you are feeling distressed in any way.

I suggest you practise the breathing exercise:

- when you wake up in the morning, before getting out of bed. What a wonderful way to welcome in the new day.

- before eating. This will effectively trigger a shift into relax mode before each meal which will help reduce digestive issues. It will also likely help you to slow your eating, and maybe encourage you to be more mindful while you are eating. You may even find that you start enjoying your food more.

- when you go to bed at night and if you wake in the middle of the night and struggle to get back to sleep. Many people have commented on how much their sleep improves once they use this technique.

Shifting from Three-year-old to Adult Mode

So, the final piece of the puzzle we posed in the first chapter has been found. We established in Chapter One that the big problem in shifting from three-year-old mode to adult mode

Learning to Chill

was the incredibly short time it took to turn on the reactive loop compared with the thinking brain. I suggested you create an image of your bratty three-year-old to help the process. Now, you have a simple breathing technique that can help create the time and space you need to allow your thinking brain to switch on.

As soon as you notice that you are in reactive mode, stop and take one or more breaths through your eyes. This will have a two-fold effect.

1. It will give your thinking brain the time it needs to switch on and start planning a response.
2. It will trigger a shift into relax mode, thus allowing you to feel better about the situation.

The effect is very much as though the world around you slows down enough for you to think about how best to tackle the situation. It really does feel as though you create time and space around you when you stop and breathe into your eyes.

IN SUMMARY

By taking control of your breath you can literally trigger a shift from distress mode to relax mode. The breathe through your eyes technique is a powerful tool to help you create the time and space you need to shift from three-year-old to adult mode when you are feeling distressed or triggered. This really is the most powerful tool I have ever found.

I would now ask you to make the commitment to yourself to regularly practise the breathing through your eyes exercise as I have recommended. Make it part of your daily routine. Use it whenever you notice yourself being reactive to help you shift into adult mode. Choose to be the adult in the room!

CHAPTER THREE

How Long is a Ball of String?

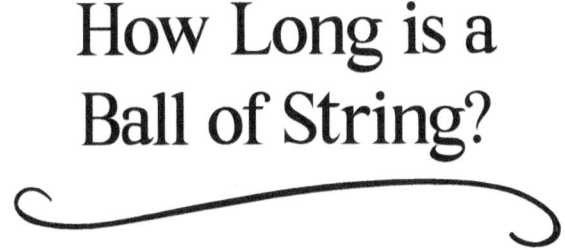

In the first two chapters I talked about how the body and brain work when you find yourself reacting to a particular situation. I've introduced you to your bratty three-year-old and your cool, calm, and collected adult.

You have learned to breathe through your eyes. This simple tool gives you the space and time to step away from your reactive behaviour and allow your adult thinking brain to take over and plan a more effective response to the situation.

Now I would like to explore with you a little more about habits – the good, the bad, and the ugly!

What is a Habit?

A habit is simply a behaviour you repeat again and again until you end up doing it without conscious thought or effort. Sometimes a habit can be useful. Sometimes a habit is not at all helpful and you suddenly realise you are acting like a bratty three-year-old.

A habit is often the automatic behaviour you fall back on when a particular situation arises. Sometimes you will trot out habits that don't work well for you when you are tired, stressed, not feeling well, distracted, and so on. Importantly, a habit is driven by your unconscious system rather than your thinking brain. The bottom line is that habits are automatic behaviours.

Now some habits are incredibly useful. Think, for example, about how automatic driving a car becomes after you've been doing it for a while. Driving requires you to use an incredibly complex set of behaviours and skills that you quite quickly learn to do without conscious thought much of the time. Hands up if you have ever driven from one place to another without remembering which route you took. I certainly have. I remember once in Cairns driving to a friend's house. There were two different routes I could take to get there. I literally either turned left or right out of my driveway. I spent the trip keeping my thinking brain busy with some problem I was having. When I arrived, I had absolutely no idea which way I'd gone. I sat in the car trying to recall any little detail that would tell me, but there was nothing I could remember that helped. I had made the trip entirely on automatic pilot. I had, of course, on automatic

How Long is a Ball of String?

pilot done everything I needed to do to arrive safely, but it was my unconscious system in charge of the journey.

You have many useful habits that work well for you. What are some of yours? Do you eat regular meals, exercise regularly, greet your friends when you see them, say please and thank you, smile back when someone smiles at you, drink water regularly through the day, clean your teeth, make meals without having to go back to the recipe, catch a ball when it's thrown to you, understand what you read, know how to write words and sentences, know where to find the letters on your keyboard when you type? Do you play a musical instrument? Your list of habits may well go on and on. In these cases, habits can be behaviours and skills you deliberately learn over time until they become automatic.

Other habits are less useful. Some clients over the years have come to me because of anger management issues, for example. They tell me that they have always quickly lashed out when they feel frustrated or feel they are being criticised. The angry outburst is a long-standing habit, an automatic response they learned early on in their lives.

I'm sure you can come up with your own personal examples of bad habits, behaviours you repeat that do not add value to your life. These may include snapping at your children, putting yourself down, agreeing to do something even when you don't have the time, running late, smoking, and so forth. What you consider to be a bad habit is up to you to decide. It is certainly not my place to decide which of your habits don't work for you.

So how and why do you create habits, whether good or bad? In essence the answer is simple.

How are Habits Formed?

Let's go back and think about your wonderful, clever, thinking brain for a moment. I often say that the thinking brain is a lazy creature, but that's not strictly true. It's more true to say that the thinking brain loves to come up with clever ideas and solutions, but doesn't want to be responsible for the tedious job of repeating the same behaviour over and over again.

Your unconscious system, on the other hand, loves routine. That part of you will happily repeat the same behaviours and thoughts again and again. It does not have the ability to do the planning and problem-solving but it's fabulous at keeping things running once it's shown what to do.

In effect, it's as though the thinking brain quickly becomes aware of any repetition of behaviour in a particular set of circumstances, and in response it effectively writes a computer program or an operations manual which the unconscious brain is then left to run whenever it's called for. So, the thinking brain does the planning and then passes over the completed program for the unconscious system to operate.

How Long is a Ball of String?

Why are Habits Formed?

There are many reasons why habits are formed. Sometimes habits are learned behaviours and skills that you enjoy or that are helpful to you. Sometimes you develop habits from watching how your parents or grandparents or friends do things, and you simply copy their behaviours until they became part of your own routine. Sometimes you might copy a less helpful behaviour simply because you don't realise there is a better option.

Sometimes you form a habit because it feels good at the time. For some of you drinking, smoking or using drugs might fit that brief. There are times when some of these habits might be seen as a means of relieving stress.

How often have you heard or said, "What a stressful day! I could really use a drink!"?

One person might see a habit as a problem, while someone else might think the same habit is perfectly okay. You are an individual, and ultimately what you decide is a good or a bad habit is entirely up to you.

How to Change a Habit

So, if a habit is an automatic behaviour that has been programmed into your brain, how do you change that habit? Well, generally it's not all that difficult, although it is effortful which means it takes work.

Many people will tell themselves, "I have to stop doing that". And what happens? They keep doing that. Why? Because they don't have a plan.

To change or stop a habit, there are a few steps to follow:

1. Think about the situation and work out what habit you want to stop or change.

2. Think about and plan what behaviour you would like to do instead in that situation.

3. Each time the situation arises, replace the old habit with the new behaviour. This will initially take attention and effort, although with consistency it will quickly become easier.

4. After trying out the new behaviour, decide how effective it was. Did it work as well as you hoped? Could you make it even better somehow? If the new behaviour worked well, simply repeat the behaviour until it becomes routine, becomes habit. If you think you could make it even better, then repeat steps 3 and 4 until you come up with something that really works for you. With practise, you have your new habit.

5. Congratulate yourself on breaking an old bad habit and forming a new good habit.

Changing a habit is initially hard work, but with consistency becomes much easier over a relatively short period of time. When I say it's hard, I don't mean that it's difficult. It's not difficult, but it does take conscious effort from you. Without conscious effort to change, you will simply continue to repeat your old habits.

How Long is a Ball of String?

Scientists have done neurological studies which show that as a new habit is formed in place of an old one, the old behaviour disappears over time. The metaphor I use for this is the ball of string metaphor.

Consider a ball of string sitting on a spool in front of you to your left (old habit). You want instead to have a ball of string on a different spool in front of you to your right (new habit). Imagine you cannot just take the string off the spool. Instead, you take the end of the string, and pull it over to the spool on the right and start to wind it into a new ball of string on the spool to the right. Part way through there is string on both spools. Habit-wise, at this stage the old behaviour is still there, but it's not as strong. The new behaviour is not completely automatic, but it's quite easy to do instead of the old habit. Once the whole ball of string is on the new spool, there is no longer any string left on the old spool. At this point, you have a brand-new habit, and the old habit has gone. That is how habits are changed. It takes time and effort, but with planning and consistency an old habit can be replaced with a new habit.

So, how long is a ball of string? Well, there's no clear answer to that. It really depends on how consistent you are in replacing your old habit with your chosen behaviour. What I can tell you is that if you consistently catch yourself and practise your new behaviour in place of your old habit, it won't take long for the new behaviour to feel comfortable. If you continue to be consistent in changing your behaviour, you will soon get to a point where you rarely slip into the old pattern at all. Almost before you know it, you won't even consider repeating your old habit. At that time, the shift is complete. A new habit of choice has been born.

Case Example

Consider the case of Diana. Diana is a young mother with a two-year-old son and a new baby. She stopped working when her son was born in order to run the house and raise her family. Diana has always been a high achiever and prides herself on looking after her family and being a good wife and mother. Diana does everything around the house herself. Her husband works long hours and lately is rarely home to help.

Recently she noticed a constant feeling of exhaustion. Caring for the house and two young children with no assistance was wearing her down. She was worried that she had begun to snap at her son when he was noisy or demanding. She was, she decided, a bad mother. She ought to be able to cope. One day, in an appointment with her GP, Diana broke down in tears. He suggested she see a psychologist.

The psychologist helped her see that she was buying into a self-limiting belief that she should be perfect. Diana was encouraged to recognise that this self-limiting belief itself was a habit that was simply not working well for her in the current situation. As a result of this habitual belief, she identified that she:

- was becoming reactive when tired and stressed
- assumed that she should be doing all the work around the house

How Long is a Ball of String?

- was task-oriented, focused on keeping the house and children immaculate
- resisted asking for assistance
- was not taking any time to look after herself
- was not spending quality time with her children, husband, family and friends.

The psychologist encouraged Diana to think about how she would have handled a similar situation when she was working. Diana recognised that she would prioritise the competing demands of her job, and delegate tasks as appropriate. Diana had an epiphany. People had been offering to help and she had been saying no because she believed it was her job to do everything. It was okay to ask for and accept help.

The psychologist encouraged her to identify her true priority when it came to her household. What might work better for her and her family?

Diana recognised that having an immaculate house was pointless if the people in the house weren't happy. What she really wanted was to create a home for her family. She decided that she would break the habit of needing everything to be perfect and focus on:

- quality time with her husband and children
- cleanliness rather than perfection in the house.

She liked the image of the bratty three-year-old and recognised that she would prefer to be the adult in the room. Since learning to remain calm and proactive, Diana has found her son to be less disruptive. She is prioritising the chores around the house and has stopped vacuuming every day. She asked her husband to take the occasional turn with the baby through the night and was pleased when he agreed to help. When she started discussing the situation with her husband, they began to make time to debrief with each other every day. They went on to arrange date nights once a month, getting her parents to babysit overnight.

Diana quickly recognised how much simpler life became when she stepped away from the habit of perfectionism. She reported feeling more content within herself and more assertive in asking for help when necessary. She noted the relationship between her husband and herself has blossomed and that he is now spending more time at home with the family. Her parents are enjoying spending more quality time with their grandchildren. Her son is happier. The baby is flourishing. She is loving spending quality time with her kids. Diana noted that the house is no longer immaculate but that it is clean.

All in all, breaking the habit of perfectionism has led to Diana feeling better about herself and her relationships than she ever has.

IN SUMMARY

Habits can be behaviours or ways of thinking, including holding onto self-limiting beliefs. A habit is simply a pattern of behaviour or thought that through repetition has become routine. It is driven by the unconscious system. Some habits are useful while other habits are not at all helpful.

What is really important is that any habit you have formed can be changed or broken. It does not matter how long it has been a habit. It only matters how you go about trying to change the unwanted habit.

Generally, changing a habit is relatively simple even though it obviously requires effort. To break an old unhelpful habit and form a brand new, more adaptive habit to replace it, you simply plan what you will choose to do instead, then put in a conscious and consistent effort to do exactly that. It will quickly become easier to make the change, and eventually the new behaviour will be your habit.

In Chapter Ten, I will discuss in more detail why some habits are more resistant to change and explore some case examples.

CHAPTER FOUR

Talk Yourself Up

In Chapter Three I talked about habits. I asked you to think about useful good habits and unhelpful bad habits. We talked about how your habits are formed and most importantly how to step away from habits that simply do not add value to your life. Generally, when your bratty three-year-old appears, he or she will trigger an unhelpful habit, because, as you know, your habits (whether good or bad) are run by your unconscious system.

Now I would like to talk specifically about how you talk to yourself when your three-year-old is in full flight. How you talk to yourself is another habit you have developed over time. I suspect you already realise that how you feel affects how you think and how you talk to yourself.

When I say talk to yourself, I mean both speaking out loud as well as conversations you hold in your head. Self-talk does not have to be out loud to have an effect, whether it be a helpful or an unhelpful effect.

The Relationship Between Emotion and Language

One habit that is extremely common is allowing your emotions to determine how you speak to yourself.

So, for example, if you're feeling:

- *depressed* you may tell yourself, "It's all too hard" or "I can't be bothered" or "My life is shit".

- *anxious* you may say to yourself, "I'm going to make a fool of myself" or "I can't breathe" or "I can't go. What if I have a panic attack?"

- *stressed* you may tell yourself, "It's all too much" or "I can't cope with this" or "It's getting out of control".

- *happy* you may tell yourself, "I love my life" or "It's such a beautiful day" or "I feel so good right now".

Most people believe that how we feel influences how we think and how we behave. Thus, if your emotions are negative, you are likely to have negative thoughts and unhelpful behaviours. It's a simple idea . . . and true as far as it goes.

Talk Yourself Up

The big problem is that such a belief creates a self-fulfilling prophecy. Simply put, once you attach a negative label to yourself, such as I'm depressed, anxious or stressed, it affects how you talk to yourself and that affects how you act.

Let us look at depression as an example.

Negative label:	I am depressed.
Possible Thoughts:	I can't talk to anyone. I'll just bring them down.
	I'm useless.
	I can't be bothered.
	My life is shit.
Possible Actions:	Lounge around in my pyjamas in front of the television all day.
	Eat junk food.
	Avoid contact with friends and family.
	Stop exercising.

So, if you're feeling depressed this is how you're going to think and act. For the most part, you just don't question it. Somehow, you have been taught that the relationship between emotion and behaviour/thought is one of cause and effect. A negative emotion causes negative thoughts and behaviours. A positive emotion causes positive thoughts and behaviours.

What most people don't fully realise is that we can indeed change our emotional response by changing our thoughts and behaviours. This simple fact is a game changer. By changing the way in which you talk to yourself, you can change how you feel. By changing what you do, you can change how you feel.

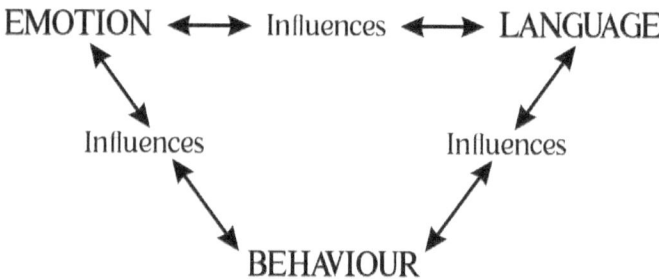

So going back to the depression example, let us consider one behavioural change you can make to help overcome depressive emotions and thoughts. That behavioural change is simply to start exercising. You already know that exercise tends to help your mood, and yet when you feel down, it's also one of the first things you stop doing.

If you are feeling depressed, I would encourage you to start the day by going for a walk. If you struggle to get motivated try planning for your morning walk the night before. Pre-planning can help you get over the lack of motivation that comes with depression. In this case, the pre-planning might include:

- deciding where you will go on your walk
- deciding how long the walk will be

- laying out your walking clothes and shoes the night before so you can easily get dressed and go when you wake up.

Mind you, in suggesting a walk, I'm being a little sneaky because when you go for your walk, you are not only getting exercise, you are also getting free Vitamin D from the sun. Vitamin D is another useful tool for helping lift depression.

We will look at other ways to combat depression in Chapter Nine. For now, I want to shift my focus back to the language you commonly use that has a negative effect on both your mood and your behaviour.

Negative Language Habits

Psychologists often refer to these negative language habits as thought distortions. A quick search of the internet found that people commonly talk about anywhere between ten and fifty different thought distortions. Also, while they will tell you what the thought distortions are, they generally don't give you specific strategies to deal with them.

Over my years of working as a clinical psychologist, I've come to realise that some types of negative language habits affect us more than other types. I will consider just four types of negative language habits that I believe sabotage your emotions and behaviours more than any other. For each type of language sabotage, I will also give you a simple, effective strategy to shift away from the sabotage and take control of your own actions and reactions, and of course your emotional response.

As you walk through life, you are surrounded by examples of people sabotaging themselves through negative language habits. In fact, every single one of us is guilty of using negative language that affects our emotions and our behaviours at least some of the time. These negative language habits are so common that most of the time you probably aren't even aware that you're sabotaging yourself with your words.

So, what are the big four negative language habits and what can you do to stop the sabotage? I will focus on all or nothing thinking, labelling, pressure language, and blaming.

All or Nothing Thinking
When you fall into the trap of all or nothing thinking you are telling yourself something absolutely must be true. The problem with all or nothing thinking is that there is no wriggle room. All means always. It means every single time without a single exception. Nothing means zero. It means never. It can never happen.

Consider walking into a shop that makes the best cakes in the world. You look in the display case and each cake looks absolutely delicious. Each cake is rich and decadent but there is one cake that draws your eyes and causes you to salivate. You make your decision.

"I want some of that cake," you say to the person behind the counter.

The person smiles at you and says, "I'm very sorry, but we only sell the whole cake which you must eat here in the store. We also have a policy that you cannot leave until you finish the whole cake. Our store is an all or nothing store."

You look at the cake you have chosen and it suddenly looks like a very big cake.

Now it's decision time. In one sitting you either eat every single crumb of that very big and rich cake or you make the choice to eat none of the cake. I'm guessing that you would struggle to eat the whole cake in one go. You might even decide that trying to eat the whole thing would make you feel sick. In that case, you might choose to walk away and eat none of the cake. It's a shame because the cake looks so very yummy. What would you decide?

Yes, all or nothing thinking really is that extreme. The words never and always are what we call absolutes. Simply put that means there is absolutely no exception. If something never happens, it literally means there is not a single example of it occurring. If something always happens, it literally means there will never be an occasion where it does not occur. In the figure below, I have set two goalposts labelled never and always. If you are using all or nothing thinking it's as though you are tying yourself to one or the other of the goalposts. Once you are tied to the post, you cannot move from that spot.

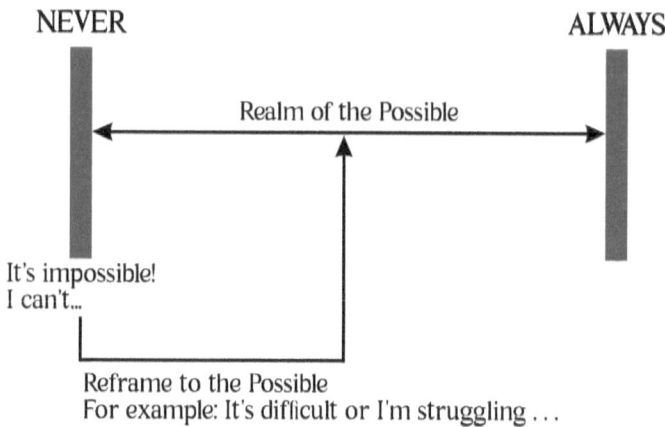

If you attach yourself to the never goalpost, you may catch yourself thinking, "It's no good. I can't do this."

Can't is short for cannot. You are telling yourself quite clearly that this is impossible.

Now many clients over the years have told me that they don't really mean that they can't do it, it's just a figure of speech. I do of course believe them. The problem is that whether they mean it or not, simply by using all or nothing language they make it true. The words create a self-fulfilling prophecy.

Why does that happen? Well, it's to do with your adult brain versus your unconscious system, particularly the reactive part of your brain. All or nothing language tends to be used as a reaction to something you are struggling with. It's reactive, therefore it's your reactive three-year-old brain that is using and buying into the language. Your adult brain may well realise that you don't really think the task is impossible, but your three-year-old self is not that sophisticated. It buys into the I can't language and simply gives up. If it's impossible, what's the point in trying after all?

Go back to the figure with the goalposts for a moment. Running between the never and always goalposts is a bar. Now, if something never happens it has a zero percent chance of happening, if something always happens it has a one hundred percent chance of happening. The bar in between the goalposts covers everything between zero and one hundred percent. It covers every bit of possibility.

I've given this bar and what it represents the rather fancy name of the realm of the possible. The bar is a continuum that goes from almost never to almost always. It covers every single bit of possibility in between never and always. What that means is that once you are somewhere on the bar, it's possible for you to move along it in either direction. You are no longer stuck.

If something is impossible or indeed if something always must happen then you have no sense of control over the outcome. The outcome is set in stone. Your actions can make no difference at all when you are dealing with never and always. The self-fulfilling prophecy is born and you are helpless in the face of it.

Help! What can I do instead? Now comes the clever bit. For you to have any control in the situation, it must be at least possible that your actions can make a difference. This is where the realm of the possible becomes your friend, your ally. To shift an all or nothing statement into the realm of the possible, you simply shift from using words like can't and always. Instead of saying, "I can't cope with this," which sits right on the never goalpost, you simply shift your language into the realm of the possible. You could say, for example, "I'm struggling with this" or "This is difficult for me". This slides you away from the goalpost and along the bar.

It doesn't have to be a shift to the positive because that might not feel believable to you. If instead of saying "I can't cope with this" you say "Of course I can cope with this" you might simply not believe it. If you don't believe it, then nothing will change.

If, on the other hand, you tend to think, "I always mess this up" you could try "I have often messed this up, but not always". However, you might again consider a shift to "I'm struggling with this" or "This is difficult for me". Personally, I like the idea of facing a challenge. It makes me want to dig in and find a way to overcome the challenge. I suspect you feel the same way.

Psychologists call this shift in your language reframing. If you reframe your all or nothing thought to recognise the difficulty of the situation, while also accepting that it is not impossible, you effectively create a challenge for yourself.

All or nothing language takes the challenge away because if something is impossible, outside our control, there is no point in fighting for the win. By reframing the language you use from the impossible to the possible, you open yourself up to the challenge of working out how to achieve your goal. Once you have a challenge you simply work out how to problem-solve it.

Body Language. I also want you to notice the physical reaction you have to the words you use. Take time to consider how your body reacts to all or nothing language. Because it's your unconscious system that's buying into the all or nothing language, you will tend to feel a physical reaction to the thought. In this case, you are likely to feel a heaviness and sinking feeling in your gut. The situation feels hopeless because you have just created a self-fulfilling prophecy and effectively told yourself that it's impossible.

Let's try a little experiment right now. See if you can think of a sentence you can relate to or have used in the past starting with "I can't . . .". Now pretend you're an actor and say it out loud (slowly and loudly) allowing yourself to feel the emotion attached to your sentence. If you can't think of anything else, simply say out loud, "I can't think of anything".

Notice the reaction your body has. Notice the sinking feeling in your gut. Notice the slight slump of your shoulders.

Now, reframe the sentence to "I'm struggling to . . .". Say that new sentence out loud.

Again, notice the sensation in your body. Notice the heaviness becomes a little lighter. Notice yourself square your shoulders as you prepare to take on this new challenge.

Did you feel the difference?

It is important that whenever you catch yourself using all or nothing language you also take notice of how your body feels. When you reframe your language to the possible, notice the feeling of heaviness decrease. Notice the other changes in how your body feels.

Noticing your physical reaction can sometimes be the first hint you pick up that you have just sabotaged yourself with the language you use. Recognising the links between your body, your brain and your language will help you step more fully into control of your own actions and reactions in whatever situation you find yourself dealing with.

Labelling

Labelling is my term for your tendency to put a label on either yourself or your habits. Labelling is not always a bad thing as sometimes it will remind you of useful habits, skills and strengths. Where labelling is unhelpful is when you maintain bad or unhelpful habits by telling yourself that is what you do.

If, for example, you have a long history of anxiety, you are likely to label yourself as anxious. Once you apply the label of anxiety, you are then more likely to call your response anxiety in any situation in which you feel uncomfortable, even if it would be completely normal and natural for absolutely anyone to feel uncomfortable in that situation.

For example, imagine going for an interview for a new job. Let's face it, going for a job interview is not a comfortable experience for most people. Most people would feel out of their comfort zone in that situation. They might even say they feel a little nervous. That is a completely natural and rational response to a job interview. Also, if you accept you are going to be uncomfortable in the interview, you are more likely to think about ways you might stay calm and make a good impression. In this situation, you are willing to put yourself out of your comfort zone in the hope of getting the job. You stay in control of your response even though you are in an uncomfortable situation.

A person with a self-label of anxiety, however, is likely to say something like, "I panic in job interviews". Panic is not rational. When you tell yourself you are panicking, you are telling yourself you are not in control and perhaps that you are not safe. Even though you may well have the strategies to manage your anxiety, when you tell yourself in the present tense that you are panicking, you literally make it true.

The problem is that when you tell yourself that this is what you do, or this is who you are, then you are not only confirming that the old habit is still your go-to behaviour in the here and now, you are also predicting that this behaviour will continue to be your habit moving forward. You are perpetuating the old habit and effectively sabotaging any efforts to change.

So, when you catch yourself putting a label on yourself or your behaviour, the trick is to put the old habit into the past. Remind yourself, "No, that is no longer me" or "No, that was my behaviour, but not anymore". Then, simply apply the techniques you already know as you continue to replace those old habits with better habits.

Pressure Language
Pressure language is my term for language you use that builds pressure, adds a burden, or creates a chore.

Get it Together Forever

If someone else tells you, "Mate, you have to apologise to her" or "You really need to think about your attitude", you might find yourself resenting their interference and resisting their advice. Let's face it, you don't really like being told what to do.

Interestingly, you are probably just as guilty of using pressure language as the next person. It is simply everywhere today. You may find yourself telling other people what you think they should do.

More importantly, I'm almost certain you sometimes tell yourself what you should be doing. You might tell yourself that you have to wash up before dinner, give Jenny a call, or even get in and sort out the bathroom cupboard. You tell yourself you have to, you must, you should, you need to, or you've got to do something.

One problem with applying pressure language to yourself is that, just as when someone else tries to tell you what you have to do, you both resent and resist it. Whatever you've told yourself must be done becomes a chore that you resent and resist.

The second issue with pressure language is that you simply don't question the idea that it must be done. You create the chore, load it on your shoulders and resent it. If you don't immediately act on it, then you may also start to feel guilty about not doing it.

Try to come up with a sentence where you are telling yourself you have got to do something. See if you can feel the weight on your shoulders, the pressure of the chore you've just created for yourself. You can?

Talk Yourself Up

So how can you reduce the pressure, get rid of the chore?

Help! What can I do instead? When you notice yourself using pressure language, stop focusing on the chore you have just created. Instead of focusing on the chore, focus on the outcome of doing the chore. Ask yourself whether this is something you want, and whether it would be useful or beneficial.

If your answer is no, then let it go. It is not something you need to do.

If your answer is yes, the next set of questions might be:

- How important is it?
- How urgent is it?
- Is it a priority?

Let's go through an example of what I mean. You have had a busy morning, You have just sat down with a book and a nice cup of tea to relax for a while before getting on with the rest of your day. As soon as you sit down, you think to yourself, "Oh I really should ring Steve".

Immediately you feel the pressure load on you. You feel resentful as you don't want to get up right now. You've just sat down to relax. You are sipping your tea but not really tasting it. Your body is tense. This is no longer the relaxing interlude you had anticipated. But wait, let's consider the issue further. You think about what you would get from ringing Steve right now. What would be the outcome?

Scenario 1: You smile as you think of speaking to him. He's always good for a chat and he's fun. Besides that, you want to talk to him about catching up tomorrow.

The Result: You decide you can read your book later. You get your phone and call Steve while enjoying your nice relaxing cup of tea.

Scenario 2: Steve has just lost his wife and while you really do want to check in with him, you know that the conversation is likely to be a bit upsetting. You decide you will ring him a little later when you have at least thirty minutes to spend supporting him.

The Result: You recognise that ringing Steve is important, but it is not immediately urgent. It would be better scheduled when you can give him your undivided attention. You plan to call him later this afternoon when you can give him your full attention. You get back to relaxing with your book and your cup of tea.

Scenario 3: You realise that you really don't want to talk to Steve because he works for a different electricity company and he's trying to get you to switch your account over to them. You are on a good plan and don't want to change. You decide to ignore his call.

The Result: In this case, calling Steve is not important or urgent. In fact, you decide it would not benefit you. You relax now that you've decided not to call him and go back to enjoying your tea and reading your book.

Talk Yourself Up

Blaming

Blaming is just what it sounds like. You react in a way you don't particularly like and put the blame for your reaction somewhere else. You might blame a person or a situation. Generally, a good tip to help recognise when you have fallen into the trap of blaming is when you talk about yourself as me rather than I.

Let's look at some examples of blaming to help you better understand:

- He yelled at me and made me cry.
- Look what you made me do.
- You make me so angry.
- Getting up in public to speak makes me so anxious.
- Grey cloudy days leave me feeling depressed.
- She's so clever, she makes me feel like an idiot.

So basically, what you are saying is that someone or something made you react in a negative or unhelpful way. Indeed, as imperfect human beings we often feel justified in blaming our response on someone else. The problem with blaming is that when you are just reacting to a situation, you are effectively in your bratty three-year-old mode. You react in an automatic, emotional way over which you have no manual control. Effectively, any time you fall into the trap of blaming, you are giving all power and control over your actions and reactions away.

Help! What can I do instead? When you speak of yourself as me in a sentence, you are having something done to you. As an example, let's look at the sentence, "You make me so angry".

In this case, because you are referring to yourself as me in the sentence, you are admitting that you have no control. Instead, you are being completely reactive to the person you are talking to. You are effectively blaming that person for your anger and in doing so you are giving that person control over your reaction.

To take back control of your reactions, it is important that you reword the sentence so that you refer to yourself as I. For example, in this case you might say, "I allowed myself to feel angry when you did that".

When you catch yourself in reactive blaming mode, take a breath in through your eyes and notice what you have just said to yourself. More than likely, you have just spoken about yourself as me. Simply start the sentence with I and take ownership of your own response. At this point, you are using your thinking brain rather than reacting as a bratty three-year-old and can choose how to respond to the situation.

Even if you change the sentence from me to I after the fact, you are no longer blaming someone else for your response. You are at least acknowledging that you had the potential to take charge of your behaviour.

If you change the sentence immediately after you make the me statement, you are choosing how to respond in the moment. Over time you will find it much easier to catch your blaming language immediately after you say it or think it. You will also find it much easier to reframe your language to get rid of the sabotage.

So, the bottom line is choose to take back control of your own response, and if necessary, be prepared to take responsibility for however you reacted in the first place. Step out of three-year-old mode and into adult mode. Be ready to apologise if you feel it would be helpful. I think you'll find, though, that when you step into adult mode and start being proactive rather than reactive, the people around you will be quite understanding of any slips you might make along the way.

IN SUMMARY

Now you know how to stop sabotaging yourself through your language. Remember, words have power. They have the power to hurt. They have the power to please. They have the power to encourage. Words can stimulate the imagination. They have the power to bring people closer or to push them away. Words can change your emotions and your behaviours. The words you choose can change the way you live your life. Words have power.

When you recognise that the words you choose to use influence your emotional and behavioural response, it can be quite a revelation. You can quite easily sabotage yourself through your words. By changing your language habits to move away from sabotage you can just as easily step into proactive adult mode.

Realistically, I believe there are just four types of language sabotage that impact on most people. These are the big four. By changing these language patterns, I am absolutely convinced, you will take a huge step forward to taking control of you – your behaviours, your emotional response, and your attitudes. So, best thought forward!

SECTION ONE WRAP-UP

You've come to the end of the first section of the book. Well done!

Now I will ask you to spend at least one week practising the tools and strategies I have outlined in Chapters One to Four.

Reflect on adult versus three-year-old behaviour. Notice your behavioural responses and choose to be the adult in the room as often as you can.

Practise breathing through your eyes and notice the space and time you create when you control your breath. Remember to practise the breathing exercise before meals. Your digestive system is designed to work best when you are at rest, so relax and enjoy your meals.

Decide which habits are not working well for you and plan what you want to do instead. Then get in and make the switch. The more consistent you are, the sooner you will create your new, helpful habits.

Finally, take notice of your thoughts and language. Recognise how your body reacts when you sabotage yourself with negative and self-limiting thoughts. Shift your language and again take note of the shift within your body.

Now get in and practise, practise, practise.

Get it Together Forever

Spend at least one week consolidating the tools and strategies you have learned in these four chapters. Make these your new habits moving forward.

SECTION TWO

Getting to Know Yourself Better

Now that you have spent a little time practising the tools and strategies in Section One, it's time to go on to the next step. If you haven't been practising the strategies I've given you so far, please stop here, go back and spend time reviewing Section One. You will only benefit from this book if you embed the strategies into your daily routine.

If you have been practising the Section One strategies, you will already be noticing a positive shift in your ability to control your own reactions. Go you! Isn't it awesome how quickly and easily you can start the transformation? You are step by step shifting towards the best version of yourself you can be.

Get it Together Forever

Section Two aids that transition by helping you get to know yourself better. By the end of this section you will see yourself in a new light. How good will it feel to treat yourself with respect and care?

CHAPTER FIVE

The Power of Two! The Power of You!

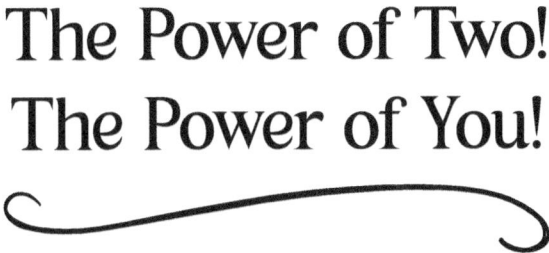

When I came up with the title of this book, *Get it Together Forever*, I was thinking only of teaching you to always have the potential to be in control of your own actions and reactions. Notice that I say always have the potential to be in control. I am not saying you will always be in control. This to me is common-sense. You are, after all, human. Please don't take offence. I'm human too. When I accept I'm only human, rather than a God or a perfect being, I also accept that I'm not perfect. I accept that I will mess up sometimes. I have also learned to step up and own my mistakes, and to step back into control of my actions as soon as I recognise that I am being reactive.

Get it Together Forever

To my mind, it's the act of taking responsibility for yourself and your actions that counts. Everyone makes mistakes, but not everyone owns their mistakes and tries to fix them. It's not the making of mistakes that is important, it's what you do when you recognise your mistake. After all, some of the best learning comes from making mistakes and having to work out how to fix things.

I hope you will also accept your humanity and everything that entails. Being human means that you can think and feel, you can empathise with others, and you can plan and problem-solve. Being human also means that sometimes you will say or think things that are not helpful. Go figure. If you're reading this, I assume you, like me, are not perfect. I also assume you want to move forward to feeling more in control of your actions and reactions.

Get it together forever does not mean learn to be perfect. It does not mean strive to be in control of everything around you. After all, realistically you cannot control everything around you. You can, however, control how you respond to what's going on around you. Get it together forever simply means take ownership of, and step into control of, your own actions and reactions.

When you get it together forever you become more resilient. Resilience is the process of adapting well in difficult or stressful situations.

Get it together forever also means stepping into the best relationship you can have with yourself. It makes sense that the most important relationship you will ever have in life is the one you have with yourself. There is not a single other person in your life who will be with you every minute of every day. No-one can truly understand the journey you have walked the way you can. So why is it often so hard to have empathy for yourself? Why do you so often criticise yourself?

There are other questions that may also apply to you. Why do you set the bar for yourself so much higher than for anyone else? Why do you think you are not good enough? Why is it so hard to find something nice to say about yourself? Why do you continue to sabotage yourself? Why do you put your needs below everyone else's? Why is it so hard for you to speak up for yourself? Why is it so hard to say no to others even when you don't really want to do what's being asked of you? Why is it so hard for you to accept help and support from other people?

Do any of these questions resonate with you? If so, I assure you that you are not alone.

Learning to like and respect yourself is harder for some people than others. Your self-esteem, your relationship with yourself, and your relationships with other people are often influenced by the self-limiting beliefs you take on from childhood.

Self-Limiting Beliefs

By definition, a self-limiting belief is one that sets a limit on how much you can grow and achieve. It keeps you stuck. Your inner critic is very competent in pointing out your self-limiting beliefs and creating doubts about your ability to succeed, or indeed, on whether you even deserve to succeed.

These self-limiting beliefs are thought to begin life as coping mechanisms that you take on as a child to safely navigate and make sense of the world as you perceive it. These beliefs are the unhelpful or sabotaging stories we hold onto about ourselves and our place in the world. You might not be aware of exactly what your sabotaging beliefs are. You simply accept without question the general viewpoint you have taken on board as a child as to who you are and how the world works. This becomes your truth. It doesn't generally occur to you to challenge those facts of life. It's just how things are. You simply continue to walk the path that other people set you on in the first place. "That's just who I am," I hear you say.

What is always true of your self-limiting beliefs is that you tend to be very receptive to any evidence that confirms the belief while completely ignoring or disregarding any evidence that disconfirms the belief. In other words, once you hold the belief to be true, you won't be told otherwise. You simply won't accept any evidence to the contrary.

These self-limiting beliefs strongly influence your less helpful habits and your reactive behaviours. Often, when you catch yourself repeating a behaviour that you keep telling yourself you want to stop, it's because that behaviour is somehow linked to one of your unhelpful beliefs.

Unfortunately, the impact of your self-limiting beliefs does not stop with you. Did you realise that the way you feel about yourself, the stories you believe about yourself, and how you treat yourself directly affects how other people treat you? If you think you're not good enough, other people will accept your self-appraisal. Some people might be nice and try to reassure you, but generally they will accept your opinion of yourself quite easily. Ultimately, if you do not think you're good enough then you won't be.

Thinking about how the stories you tell yourself influence how other people treat you, stop and consider the energy that an extremely depressed person puts out. I'm sure you have seen someone in your lifetime of whom you think, "They suck the energy out of the room".

You don't try to tell them they are not depressed. It's obvious they are depressed. You can sense it. You can feel it.

How you feel about yourself is also reflected out into the universe for other people to pick up on and react to. It's reflected in many ways, some obvious, some subtle. It's in your body language, your voice, your actions and reactions. It's in your attitude. Whether people are aware of picking up on the signals you're broadcasting or not, there is no doubt that what we put out to the universe impacts how other people respond to us.

Whether or not you are always hard on yourself, I am sure you have beliefs particular to you that influence your reactive behaviours and decisions.

If you hold the belief that you do not deserve to be financially successful, you will not be financially successful. This is because you sabotage your efforts to make good money and because other people will accept your self-limiting belief and not offer you good money. I can remember a time when I would apologise for the amount I charged for a neuropsychological assessment. This often resulted in clients deciding it was too expensive and choosing not to pay the money. As I overcame the self-limiting belief relating to the value of my services, I raised my fee by $700 without apologising and clients paid without question.

If you hold the belief that your only value is in what you do for others, you are likely to put everyone else's needs before your own. If this is you, you may struggle to accept help or support from others. Instead, you see yourself as the go-to person amongst your family and social circle. You may find yourself in relationships or friendships that are quite one-sided. You give and they take.

But what if things could be different? What if you did not have to continue to buy into your original set of self-limiting beliefs? What if you could deliberately and proactively choose your own path? Yes, it is possible to choose your own path!

Choosing to Change

I know from years of experience working with a wide range of clients that it's never too late to change your beliefs and choose a new path. Age does not have to be a barrier. The amount of time you have spent maintaining your self-limiting beliefs does not have to be a barrier. You simply need to believe in your ability to exchange your self-limiting beliefs for more adaptive beliefs. Creating more adaptive beliefs might start with the decision to respect and value yourself.

I want to take a moment to clarify a point that some people struggle with. Respecting and valuing yourself is not the same as being selfish. Selfish people tend only to think about themselves. Selfish people tend to be takers and not givers. It is likely that you are not selfish. You are a caring human being. Helping other people may even be a core value in your life. What I am suggesting is that caring about yourself does not suggest you do not care about other people. Let's face it, if you make sure you are okay, then you are better placed to help and support those you care about. If you put yourself last and then crash and burn, the value you give to those you care about is less than your best. Think about that. It's an important point.

Now I should put in a warning here.

Warning: Improving your relationship with yourself may change your relationships with others.

This is something I often see occur with my clients. As their relationships with themselves improve and they start treating themselves with care and respect, many other people in their lives tend to begin treating them with more respect and regard also. Many of my clients over the years have commented on how much their relationships with people they care about blossom as they learn to appreciate themselves. They finally appreciate the essence of a good relationship is reciprocity, which simply means there is give and take on both sides. The relationship is equal. It is effectively a partnership of sorts.

Not all relationships blossom, however. Selfish people who are only in your life because you are a giver tend to disappear when you start valuing and respecting yourself. They are not interested in a reciprocal relationship. These people are only interested in what's in it for them. They are the people in your life who tend to never be there when you need them but will always be there with their hands out if they want something from you.

So, how do you step into the best relationship you have ever had with yourself and people you care about? I'm glad you asked, because I have another metaphor that I believe you will find incredibly helpful.

In Section One, we largely focused on the small part of your unconscious self, the reactive loop, responsible for your automatic negative reactions. For that reactive response I used the analogy of the bratty three-year-old. Now, though, I would like to introduce you to another way of thinking about the thinking brain versus the entire unconscious system. It's time to learn to appreciate your unconscious system and all it does for you. The unconscious system is, after all, a vital part of you. You wouldn't be alive without it. Realistically, to function as you, you need both the conscious and the unconscious systems working as a team.

Meet the Team

Let's think about you as a business or a company. The Company of You! It has a nice ring to it, don't you think? In your company you have the director or the boss who decides how the company should be run and you have the office staff or worker who largely is responsible for keeping the company running smoothly. You already know the first half of your team.

The Boss
In many ways, the boss is the truest reflection of who you are. The boss takes in information, solves problems, makes plans, decides what needs to be done when, and manages and trains the staff. The boss provides the unique vision and ethos of the company, based on your personality, moral code and the value system that defines what is important to you.

The boss is able to sit back and observe what's going on both within yourself and in the outside world. Some of you might have heard about the observing self, which is often talked about in mindfulness and meditation exercises. Sitting back and noticing how you are feeling, how your body is reacting to your thoughts and emotions, is a skill you can learn. Many psychologists talk about the thinking brain and the observing self as two separate parts, and I agree that observing (noticing) and thinking are quite different skills.

It makes sense to me, though, that if the boss is going to be in charge of the whole company, that part of you not only has to make the decisions and rules, it also has to observe how the company as a whole is faring. The information gained from noticing or observing is incredibly useful for helping you recognise triggers, reactions, helpful or unhelpful habits, and even how other people are reacting in a situation.

In many ways the boss is you, the part of you that notices what is going on and makes conscious choices about what to do. In effect, the boss is in charge of making executive decisions and is responsible for creating the operations manual that the worker uses for the day-to-day running of the company. The boss is also responsible for updating the manual, when necessary, so the worker is following the correct procedures.

What the boss doesn't like so much is constant repetition and routine. The day-to-day running of the company is left almost entirely in the hands of the worker. The boss doesn't need to know how the communications systems work or how to keep the plumbing functioning optimally. The boss doesn't have conscious access to many of the automatic tasks the worker takes charge of. The boss might say, "Do this", but it's up to the worker to make it happen. The worker keeps the company running smoothly and efficiently.

The Worker
The worker is the other side of the coin, your unconscious self, the part of you that manages all the routine day-to-day tasks that keep your whole system running. The worker is incredibly hard-working, conscientious, loyal and reliable.

The worker keeps your entire body functioning – breathing, heart beating, blood flowing, and so on. The worker is also in charge of carrying out many simple and complex tasks that you might think of as automatic behaviours or habits. The worker is responsible for maintaining the routines because the boss gets bored with repetition, whereas the worker thrives on it. The worker can carry out complex tasks (think driving for example) but is not capable of making independent decisions around new behaviours. In other words, the worker does exactly what the boss has instructed (even if you're not aware of having given the instructions). Think of these instructions as your operations manual. The boss, of course, is responsible for writing the manual and familiarising the worker with any new instructions.

Sometimes the manual may contain very old instructions that you learned when you were a young child. Some helpful behaviours you may have learned from your parents or other people around you include tying your shoelaces, getting dressed, cleaning your teeth, making toast, buttering bread, saying thank you, and the list goes on. Some habits you learned as a child may be less helpful. Sometimes the reactive behaviours you bring out when you feel stressed or threatened began with your parents. In those cases, it may never have occurred to you that you can change those habits.

If you follow this logic through, it becomes clear that the worker is not at fault for trotting out habits that you may not particularly like. The worker is simply doing their job to the best of their ability – following the manual they have been given. The worker does not know the difference between helpful and unhelpful habits. It's the job of the boss to notice the unhelpful habits and decide what to do about them. Perhaps it might be a good time to update your manual?

While I've already talked about how to change a habit, I would like you to think about how that fits in with this new idea of rewriting the manual when the old instructions are no longer working for you. The rewriting can address reactive behaviours, self-limiting beliefs, and sabotage through language. These are all examples of unhelpful habits.

When clients think about changing old patterns of thought and behaviour, they often say to me, "I've been doing that all my life. It'll take a long time for me to change."

My response goes something like this: "If you tell yourself it'll take a long time to break that habit, then you're right. It will. Not because the habit has to take a long time to change, but rather because you are setting up a self-fulfilling prophecy when you tell yourself it will take a long time. In a sense you are labelling and using all or nothing thinking when you tell yourself you have a long-standing habit that you cannot change quickly."

I'll give you an example to demonstrate how quickly you can adapt. Many of you will have driven a particular car for quite a long time. Driving becomes automatic. You get behind the wheel of another car and the indicators are on the other side of the steering wheel. Now, if a long-term automatic behaviour must take a long time to change, you would naturally continue to turn on the windscreen wiper instead of the indicator. I bet you don't do that for long, though. My guess is that the first time you drive this new car you will get it wrong somewhere between one and three times. Quickly the boss jumps in and tells the worker, "Okay, we have to modify the instruction manual slightly for this car. All you need to remember is that the indicators and windscreen wipers are on the opposite sides in this car." A note is made in the manual, and the worker quickly adapts to the new situation.

That ability to adapt is one of the things that helped human beings survive against the odds. It's one of your greatest strengths.

That ability to adapt tells me that any habit, no matter how long-standing or entrenched, can be changed relatively quickly if the boss does the appropriate training and updates the manual properly. The worker will respond well to good training. It's really up to the boss to do the planning, do the training, remind the worker of the new response when necessary, then trust the worker to take the training on board and run with it.

Now I would like you to think about the culture of your company, including the relationship between the two distinctly different parts of you who make up your company

The Relationship
The company is made up of the boss and the worker. When the relationship between the boss and the worker is a good one the company runs smoothly. Think about workplaces you may have known. Think about jobs you've had that you've enjoyed. I am certain that in these jobs you had a good boss and the culture in the workplace was one of appreciation and respect. It was supportive and encouraging.

Now think about jobs that you didn't like, jobs in which you didn't feel appreciated. This may very well be because the culture in that workplace was toxic. It's a well-known saying that a fish rots from the head down, and that's very true of a toxic work environment as well. The culture of a workplace is created at the top. The boss is responsible for the workplace culture. If the boss is organised and fair, as well as supportive and encouraging, then the culture of the workplace is likely to be a good one. In this case, the business is likely to be successful.

If, however, the boss is unreasonable and blames the workers when things don't go right, the culture is likely to be toxic – a culture of blame. We've all experienced or known of a toxic work environment.

When you get annoyed with yourself for repeating a bad habit, or when your inner critic is in full flight, it's as though the boss is blaming the worker for simply doing their job. Think of that hard-working, loyal, and reliable worker who always tries to do the best job they can for the company. When you, the boss, criticise or blame the worker for not doing the right thing it's as though you are beating the worker with a big stick or a whip. Think of the poor worker, silently suffering, not understanding what they did to deserve such abuse. There's a sense of helplessness and hopelessness. The worker is, after all, simply doing what the boss has instructed. What is a poor worker to think and do when they get abused for simply doing their job to the best of their ability? It's just not fair! You, the boss, are creating a toxic work environment.

Stop for a moment and reflect on where the responsibility for your behaviour lies. If your worker is repeating a habit you don't like, it suggests that you, the boss, have not yet instituted the changes you want. You have not yet informed the worker of the change and updated the operations manual. It takes a little time to update the manual and train the worker. So, stand up and tell yourself, "The buck stops here!" It's an old saying, but a good one. If you don't like something about yourself or your behaviour, don't beat up on your worker. Instead take responsibility for your own actions and reactions – plan a new strategy, update the manual, train the worker, and move forward. Create a positive and supportive work environment for your company and indeed for yourself.

Instead of beating up on yourself, recognise how important both parties in the company are when it comes to making the company run smoothly. Imagine standing side by side, boss and worker, both appreciating and respecting the other, both working hard in their own ways to make the company a success. Neither can operate the company alone. It is a team effort. Appreciate your team. Appreciate your worker. Appreciate yourself. Mutual respect and appreciation lead to a positive culture within your company. A positive culture leads to success and growth.

Stop and visualise the two distinct and indispensable parts that make up the company of you. The boss is intelligent and clever – able to adapt to new situations and make plans to move ahead. The worker is not imaginative, but is hard-working, reliable and loyal.

Imagine them both, standing together. Imagine turning to your worker and saying, "Thank you for all your hard work".

Get it Together Forever

In fact, try looking at your worker in the mirror and saying thank you out loud.

Get ready to have the best relationship with yourself you have ever known. Step away from your self-limiting beliefs. Silence your inner critic. You are fabulous. Believe in the power of two. Believe in you.

CHAPTER SIX

Get it Together Forever

This chapter marks the end of Section Two. As you stop and reflect on the ideas, tools and strategies I've given you in the past two sections, you are possibly thinking that it's all so simple. Well, you would be right. It is simple. You might even be thinking that what I am suggesting is obvious, to which I would reply, "So why aren't you doing it already?" I think that is part of the beauty of this system. There is nothing in it that is likely to feel particularly uncomfortable. The concepts are all familiar, so it's not difficult to put them into practice, although putting them into practice will require effort on your part. To my mind, this system also falls under the banner of common-sense, which I'm sure you would agree is far from common.

Get it Together Forever

Before you go on to Section Three of the book, please spend at least a further week putting the ideas and strategies from Sections One and Two into use. Read through the strategies as often as you need in order to understand them and embed them in your daily life. You will be forming new adaptive habits. If you put the effort into creating these new habits, you will notice significant changes in the way you deal with all the stuff life throws at you.

The information I have given you so far in this book will allow you to make incredible changes in the way you manage stressful situations, and indeed the general pressures of life itself.

You will realise that you cannot control everything around you. When it comes down to it, you are only ever in control of your own response to any situation. You cannot control other people. By responding in a proactive and thoughtful way, however, you can often influence how other people respond. In other words, when you respond proactively in a situation, you may well be able to influence what is happening around you even if you cannot directly control it.

It's interesting how much in your life changes when you step into your adult mode instead of responding like a three-year-old. For some of you, the information in these two sections will be all you need to get it together forever.

With some effort and commitment from you, I fully expect you to improve your sense of control, your resilience in the face of challenges, and your level of contentment and emotional well-being. They say that practice makes perfect, but as I do not believe in perfection as a goal, let me just say, "Practice leads to the forming of new habits". Consistency is the key.

I want to share another metaphor that recently occurred to me. Suppose you decide to grow a vegetable garden. It requires water and fertiliser in order to produce good quality vegetables. If you buy the fertiliser, but fail to fertilise and water your garden, the vegetables will not grow. If, however, you make the effort to both water and fertilise you will have a good crop of vegetables.

Reading this book is a good first step, but to grow into the best version of yourself you can be, an initial effort of consistently using the tools and strategies is required. Before you know it, however, these new strategies will become your new habits. While putting these strategies into practice, please remember to be kind to yourself. Remember that you, the boss, are in the process of training your worker in a new system or set of strategies. Over time, you will rewrite your own manual, and gradually the worker will become so familiar with the new strategies that they won't have to refer back to the manual. At the point that the new strategies become completely automatic, new habits have formed.

Your progress may look something like this:

Before you start to change the unhelpful behaviour:

> A situation arises, your old habit kicks in, your three-year-old kicks off.

You decide to change the unhelpful behaviour and plan a new behaviour:

> A situation arises, your old habit kicks in, your three-year-old kicks off, you realise you are being reactive, breathe through your eyes, and step into your new planned behaviour.

After you have been practising your new behaviour for a few days:

> A situation arises, you catch yourself before your old habit kicks in, breathe through your eyes, and step into your new planned behaviour.

A little time later, after consistently putting new behaviour in place:

> A situation arises, you breathe through your eyes, and step into your new planned behaviour.

In a time not too far away:

> A situation arises and you automatically trot out your new habit.

Remember, also, that changing your old habits doesn't have to take a lifetime. It's not the length of time you have had the habit that counts, it's the consistency of the effort you put in to change.

Integration of Sections One and Two

To start, let me remind you of the framework upon which the strategies rest.

The Framework
In essence, I suggested you consider yourself in two parts:

1. The conscious system, or the boss, that is made up of the thinking brain and the observing self.

    a. The thinking brain is the part that plans and problem-solves and allows you to be proactive in any given situation. It allows you to be the adult in the room.

    b. The observing self is the part of you that notices how and what you are feeling. It incorporates each of your senses, and feeds information to the thinking brain.

2. The unconscious system, or the worker, automatically runs your entire physical being and is responsible for driving the reactive loop that is automatically engaged when we are triggered by a difficult situation. When the reactive loop is triggered, you may well find yourself acting like a bratty three-year-old.

    The autonomic nervous system is part of the unconscious system. The autonomic nervous system has two modes:

    a. Distress mode is often referred to as fight or flight mode. When you are distressed your body is in a heightened state of awareness. You may feel anxious, scared or stressed. When your body stays in distress mode for long periods of time it can lead to digestive issues such as indigestion and reflux. It can affect your immune system, your sleep patterns, and raise your blood pressure.

b. Relax mode is the ideal state for you to be in when there is no physical danger present. An easy way to shift from distress mode to relax mode is to change your breathing from fast and shallow to deep, diaphragmatic breathing. Instead of teaching the traditional method of diaphragmatic breathing I taught you to breathe through your eyes.

The Steps of Change

Remember that habits are not difficult to break. It's merely a matter of putting the effort in and being consistent with noticing and changing your behaviours. The steps are simple.

1. Notice when you start falling into an old unwanted pattern of behaviour. *Observing self in action. The boss is on the job.*

2. Breathe through your eyes to allow your thinking brain time to wake up. *The boss is on the job and starting to make a plan.*

3. Decide how you would like to respond. *The boss decides on a strategy.*

4. Put that new behaviour into place. *The boss starts training the worker.*

5. Repeat steps 1 to 4 as necessary. *The boss rewrites the manual and continues to train the worker until the worker masters the new strategy.*

Which Habits to Change

You have good habits that work well for you, and unhelpful habits that don't. I'm relatively sure that you are aware of which habits don't work for you. I also believe that you are now capable of making plans to change those habits that no longer work for you.

While I was talking about habits, I spoke about the fact that the language you choose to use can strongly influence your emotional state as well as your actions and reactions. We humans have a bad habit of sabotaging ourselves with the language we use. I took you through the four most influential language habits that serve to sabotage you:

1. ***All or nothing thinking.*** When you use all or nothing thinking you are generally telling yourself the situation is impossible. I suggested that you shift your language to reflect that while the situation might be difficult it is not actually impossible.

2. ***Labelling.*** Labelling is a special form of all or nothing thinking in which you put a label on yourself or your behaviours, thus perpetuating your old story. The trick here is to shift the label into the past, acknowledging it as a past habit rather than a current habit.

3. ***Pressure language.*** When you use pressure language, such as have to, need to, should, etc., you instantly create a chore for yourself. Instead, I suggest you look

at the likely outcome of doing the task and make a conscious choice as to whether it would be beneficial. If no, then scrap the idea. If yes, then decide how important and urgent it is. Plan when to do it and get on with your day.

4. *Blaming*. Blaming is when you put the responsibility for your behaviour on someone else's shoulders. You abdicate control of your own actions and reactions as soon as you blame someone or something else. I suggest you step into your adult mode and take responsibility for your own actions even if you don't approve of them. If you don't approve of your actions or behaviours, choose to change them – rewrite the manual and train the worker accordingly.

Contentment

Before I finish with this chapter, I want to briefly mention one final concept. Many people are taught to focus on happiness as their goal in life, as their measure of success. My response to that is to remind you that it is not possible to be happy all the time. Maximising your moments of happiness is reasonable and of course desirable, but please don't expect to be happy all the time. Instead, I suggest focusing on a slightly different concept – contentment.

Learn to be content being you. You can be content within yourself even when you are sad. I believe contentment is contained within you and reflects your relationship with yourself. As you go through this journey and step into your inner adult, I urge you to focus on finding contentment within yourself. Develop a positive work culture within yourself and let the company of you thrive.

Practise, Practise, Practise

As we come to the end of the first two sections, I want to again emphasise the importance of practising the techniques and strategies included within. These few simple strategies are the foundation of change.

Ask yourself, "Am I prepared to step up and be responsible for my own actions and reactions? Am I ready to step up and take control of my life?"

If the answer to these questions is yes, then do yourself a huge favour and go back to the beginning and continue practising this common-sense approach to resilience.

Before moving on to Section Three, please spend at least one week practising the strategies in these first two sections. Make these strategies your own. Build them into life-long habits. Until you start to embed these core strategies you will not really know which chapters in Section Three will be of particular use to you.

I would also suggest that you occasionally take time to stop and notice the strategies you are using, even after they become habits. By doing so, you will always have access to the helpful strategies if your world suddenly turns pear-shaped.

What I promise you is that if you follow this common-sense system and embed these core strategies, you will always have the capacity to be in control of your own actions and reactions. That, of course, is not to say you will always be in control of your own actions and reactions. You are, after all, only human. All humans slip up sometimes. So be kind to yourself. Be resilient. Forgive yourself for being human and choose to learn from your mistakes.

When you feel confident that your revised operations manual is well on the way to being completed, when you find it easy to step into your new behaviours of choice, then go to Section Three of this book.

The chapters in Section Three are each devoted to a particular issue. It may be that after practising the techniques from Sections One and Two you no longer feel the need to explore further. If, however, you are still struggling with old patterns or beliefs take a look at Section Three. You probably won't need to read all the chapters so feel free to focus on those you feel are of most relevance to you.

Finally, to wrap up Section Two, let me say congratulations on getting this far. Make use of the tools and strategies, and enjoy the process of getting to know and respect yourself. Good luck with your journey. May you grow to be content within yourself.

SECTION THREE

You Want More?

It is said that if you know your enemies and know yourself, you will not be imperilled in a hundred battles; if you do not know your enemies but do know yourself, you will win one and lose one; if you do not know your enemies nor yourself, you will be imperilled in every single battle.

— Sun Tzu, The Art of War

You may be wondering why I started this section with a quote attributed to the ancient Chinese general and philosopher, Sun Tzu. I think this quote is particularly apt. What it is saying is that if you know yourself and your enemy – such as stress, anxiety, or depression – you can win every battle. If you know yourself but you do not have knowledge of your enemy, you will win and lose equally. If you know neither yourself nor your enemy you will lose every battle. This makes sense and supports the old adage that knowledge is power.

So having worked your way through Section One and then Section Two, you have a much better understanding of yourself. I trust you are feeling more resilient, more in control of your own actions and reactions than you were previously. I hope you finally feel you know yourself and that you are treating yourself with more appreciation and respect.

In Section Three, I am going to focus on giving you more detailed information about the enemy and how to fight it. I will specifically target common issues that can be difficult to shift for one reason or another. It may be that you are drawn to one or more of the chapters I have included here. I am going to give you more information about these common issues as well as a few more strategies and tools to use as you need.

The idea in this section is to choose the chapters that address your needs. If you have never suffered from anxiety you may choose not to read the chapter on anxiety. The book is in your hands and the decision is yours.

So what do the different chapters cover?

- Chapter Seven deals with anxiety.

- Chapter Eight deals with stress.
- Chapter Nine deals with depression.
- Chapter Ten deals with stubborn and complex habits.

These extra chapters provide information that may be useful in dealing with those stubborn labels you continue to apply to yourself. Read as many or as few of the chapters as you feel apply to you or interest you.

I will again mention that this book is not designed to replace therapy with a qualified professional. If you continue to have significant issues with your mental health, I strongly urge you to seek professional assistance.

CHAPTER SEVEN

What If?

Do you think of yourself as anxious? Are you a worrier? If the answer to these questions is yes, you are certainly not alone. A quick internet search suggested that in Australia around 14% of the population has been diagnosed with an anxiety disorder. That's one person in every seven who has an official diagnosis of anxiety. In my experience, however, there are many more people who may not warrant a formal diagnosis, but who still experience anxiety, excessive worry, or even what they might think of as panic in a range of situations. Without doing a file review, I can confidently say that the majority of my clients over the years initially presented with high levels of anxiety symptoms (and no . . . not just because they had to deal with me).

Often, when people struggle with all the stuff that life throws at them, their levels of anxiety and stress rise also. So, what's going on? Why do you feel anxious when you feel overwhelmed? Why do you spend so much time worrying about what might happen? Why do you find yourself withdrawing from, or avoiding, certain situations? How does anxiety do such a good job of weaselling its way into your life?

In fact, let's cut straight to the chase and ask what is this thing called anxiety anyway? Then I'll explore how anxiety develops and how it is maintained. Finally, I'll discuss strategies you can use to stop feeling anxious.

What is Anxiety?

According to the Diagnostic and Statistical Manual of Mental Disorders (Fifth Edition), also known as the DSM-5, anxiety is *anticipation of future threat.* It goes on to say that anxiety is *often associated with muscle tension and vigilance in preparation for future danger and cautious or avoidant behaviours.* Okay, so far so good, but you might ask why anxiety is such a debilitating condition if it's just about being cautious and avoidant of dangers. That just sounds like common-sense.

If there is a real, physical threat to you, then your fight or flight reflex would kick in and hopefully get you out of harm's way. That is a normal and adaptive human response to real danger. It's the reflex that allowed mankind to survive against bigger, stronger predators. I spoke about fight or flight at some length in Chapter Two.

What If?

If you are out on the town and a big brawl kicks off on the street ahead of you, it is likely that you won't just walk through the middle of it. You may choose to call the police. You may choose to walk away so you don't get caught up in it. Either way, although you are likely to be feeling your fight or flight reflex kick in, and you are probably choosing to stay safe and err on the side of caution, you may not actually be feeling anxious. If you follow your instinct and respond to this situation in a cautious and sensible way that keeps you safe, what you are feeling and the way you are reacting are normal responses to a dangerous and threatening situation. You may tell yourself you feel anxious in this situation if you have a history of anxiety, but what's important to recognise in this case is that it is a normal human response to avoid putting yourself in physical danger.

The difficulty with anxiety is that it's not about your response to real and present danger. It's your response to an imagined threat. When I say imagined threat, I'm not talking about mythical monsters, I'm talking about your mind's tendency to imagine the worst-case scenario. The problem of course is that once you imagine the worst-case scenario that's what you focus on – you begin to create a self-fulfilling prophecy.

Many people focus on the idea that when you feel anxious, you don't feel safe. That, of course, is likely part of what you are experiencing when you feel anxious, however, I think what's most important is the idea that you do not feel in control. The reason I believe that your sense of control outweighs your sense of safety is simply that you are able to put yourself in a potentially unsafe situation while maintaining control of your reaction, but if you do not feel in control of your own actions and reactions and you find yourself in a dangerous situation, you are probably going to be quite anxious.

Imagine you are out bushwalking and while you are taking photos your child slips away from you. You hear them call out in distress, and you run to find them. When you find them, they are frozen on the path with a snake curled up in front of them and starting to look threatening. You realise that sudden movements are likely to startle the snake into striking. You take a deep breath and calm yourself. You quietly tell your child to stand still, don't move, that you will come and get them. The child relaxes at your voice but keeps their eyes on the snake. You glide to the child and slowly and gently pick them up. Then you quietly and slowly move away from the snake. In this situation you and your child are in danger, but because you remain in control of your own actions you react appropriately to keep you both safe.

Imagine, however, if you did not feel in control of your own actions in this situation. If you felt both unsafe and not in control. If you allowed the panic to rise, how might your child react? If they also panicked, the outcome might not be such a good one.

That, of course, is an example of a real situation in which danger exists. But you can create just as strong a sense of being unsafe and lacking control in your imagination.

Stop for a moment, and just think about the last time you felt anxious, worried, or panicky when there was not a real physical threat right in front of you. You were possibly

What If?

thinking about a situation that left you feeling uncomfortable. What was the main issue you were grappling with? Was it a sense of not feeling safe? Was it a sense of not feeling in control of the situation? Was it a combination of both? What was it that you thought might happen if you put yourself in that situation? When we feel anxious, we do a great job of bringing out the "What if . . ." statements. "What if I have a panic attack because there are so many people on the train, and I can't get off? I just can't put myself in that situation!"

I have noticed that when I ask my anxious clients why a situation causes them anxiety, many of them struggle to say exactly what they are afraid will happen. Many will say that they are avoiding a situation because they might have a panic or anxiety attack. So, in effect they are reporting that the situation makes them anxious because they might become anxious in the situation. Does that sound familiar to you? I would imagine that if anxiety is still a concern for you after practising the strategies outlined in the first two sections of this book, you understand exactly how my clients feel. To a large extent, anxiety is the fear of the fear.

I often use a metaphor of blowing up a red balloon. I choose red to symbolise danger, but if danger to you is better represented by a different colour, then please imagine your balloon in that colour instead. So, when you first come across a situation that causes you a sense of discomfort, it's as though you blow the first lot of air into the balloon. If you start to feel anxious at the idea of facing the situation again, then you blow more air into the balloon, and the balloon gets bigger. If you start systematically avoiding the situation because it makes you uncomfortable, the balloon keeps getting bigger and bigger until eventually it's the size of a house. So now the big red balloon is pretty much all you can see in your mind's eye, and thus it occupies a large part of your attention. At this point it's likely that your anxiety has generalised to a range of other situations as well. You will probably be avoiding all sorts of situations as your anxiety feels overwhelming and you feel less and less in control of your own response. Anxiety is now interfering with you getting on with your life.

You find yourself sitting there looking at this immense red balloon and feeling completely overwhelmed by it. But what is inside the balloon? How substantial is it really? If you can find a way to pop the balloon, what will be left? Let me remind you that the balloon contains only what you breathed into it – it's full of air. I often suggest it's full of hot air. In other words, the threat the balloon represents is not real.

Your anxiety is due to an imagined threat – in fact, it's often due to a threat you actually struggle to identify. It seems to be the expectation of feeling fearful that leads to you feeling fearful. If I tried to sell you that concept, you wouldn't even consider buying. "What?" you'd say. "You expect me to buy into being afraid of being afraid? What do you take me for?"

But anxiety is a better salesperson (or should that be sales entity?) than I am. Anxiety is sneaky. I really do mean that. Anxiety is very, very sneaky. It's as though it whispers in your ear and feeds that natural human instinct to be wary of danger. It undermines your confidence and convinces you that you cannot cope with a situation. Anxiety creates a cycle that involves your unconscious system in the form of the body (fight or flight mode), your brain (reactive thoughts), and your behaviour (how you act). As you go round and round the cycle, the anxiety continues to grow and generalise (think big red balloon) until it is having a huge impact on your life. Some people get to the point where they don't feel safe leaving home. Some people don't even feel safe at home unless there's someone there with them.

So how does the anxiety cycle work?

The Anxiety Cycle

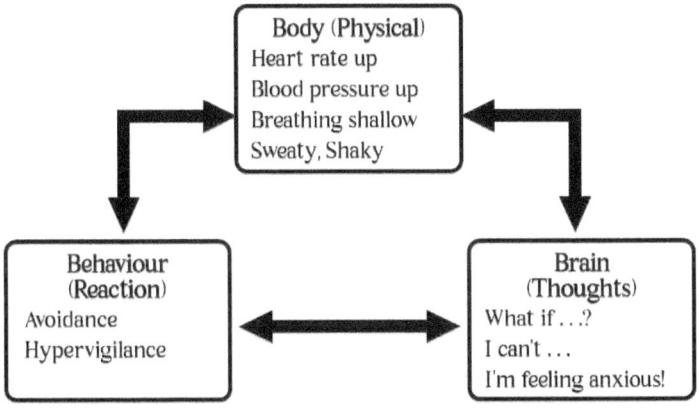

The anxiety cycle can start anywhere, although it tends to start with either a negative thought or a physical reaction which you interpret as an anxious response. Notice that I've made the arrows in the figure bi-directional, so that they point in both directions. I did that because any part of the anxiety cycle can influence any other part. Negative thoughts can lead to a physical shift into fight or flight mode. Shortness of breath can be interpreted as a symptom of anxiety and cause the brain to look for a reason to be fearful, triggering negative thoughts. Avoiding a situation can generate negative thoughts, causing you to label the situation as one that makes you anxious.

The physical symptoms I've listed in the anxiety cycle diagram are typical of the physical changes you experience when your body shifts into fight or flight mode. If you have experienced anxiety, I imagine you've noticed your breathing and heart rate change. You are probably aware that your blood pressure gets higher when you are anxious. You may well have experienced shakiness and sweaty palms when highly anxious. Additionally, an adrenalin surge gives an extra boost to your power and speed. Blood flow is focused in your big muscles, particularly in your arms and legs, to increase your strength to either fight or run away. Fight or flight is all about boosting power, and it is incredibly useful to have that power when you are under actual physical threat.

Working in hospital settings, I noticed a relatively high occurrence of anxiety in people with chronic medical conditions, particularly those that impact on their breathing or their heart. People with Chronic Obstructive Pulmonary Disease (COPD), for example, have a high incidence of anxiety and panic. COPD often causes shortness of breath, which can be interpreted by your brain as a signal of danger in which case a shift into fight or flight mode occurs. This can lead to an anxiety or panic attack unless you are able to remind yourself that the shortness of breath is simply a symptom of your medical condition. One of the big problems

What If?

for people with COPD who develop anxiety is that exercise tends to trigger the anxiety response due to the onset of breathing difficulties. As a result, some sufferers start avoiding exercise, which then leads to an exacerbation of their breathing issues as they get physically weaker and potentially more overweight. It can be a vicious cycle.

Anxiety is a vicious cycle regardless of any underlying medical conditions. The anxiety cycle is most likely to be triggered by either a thought or a physical sensation. Let us imagine you are triggered when you get the text reminding you of tomorrow's dentist appointment. You suddenly remember that you don't know this dentist. They might not understand you sometimes struggle to breathe when they keep your mouth open too long. You immediately feel your heart pound and your breathing change. You begin to worry that you might not cope and the new dentist might not notice your distress. Your old dentist who has just retired was gentle and able to relax you. What if this new one is some kind of sadist or just task-focused? Your breathing is getting faster and you feel your palms start to sweat. You tell yourself that it's important that you go this time because it's been more than a year since your last check-up and you've been noticing some bleeding in your gums. Your thoughts start to run on. What if I need more than a check-up? How will I cope if I have to be in the chair for more than an hour? I can't do it. I'll end up having a panic attack and freaking out. Your hands start shaking and you feel as though you can't breathe. You reach for the phone and text back, "No" to whether or not you plan to attend the appointment. The relief you feel is incredible as you avoid the terrifying situation. You choose to ignore your bleeding gums for now, avoiding also the thought of what might be causing the problem.

In this case, the thought triggers the physical reaction which leads to more reactive thinking which leads to greater physical distress, until the situation becomes so uncomfortable you choose to avoid it by cancelling the appointment and ignoring the signs that the appointment was perhaps important. Having decided to cancel the appointment you immediately feel less uncomfortable, and this leads to a flawed piece of logic which goes something like this: If I feel so much better now that I've decided not to go to the dentist then the situation must be very scary and dangerous. I couldn't cope with it.

This is flawed logic because it is built on assumption rather than experience. You are imagining the worst-case scenario and effectively deciding that the worst-case scenario is the reality of the situation and that you would absolutely not be able to cope with it. A case of all or nothing thinking.

Most people who get anxious don't just get anxious about one particular situation. Anxiety tends to generalise as you both train your unconscious (the worker) to focus on the worst-case scenario and feel less and less in control of your own response. When your anxiety gets worse your tendency to avoid various situations also increases.

Once the anxiety cycle is established it maintains itself quite effectively. In maintaining itself, it also consolidates the stories and increases its power over you. At this point, you have probably applied a label to yourself. You start to

What If?

tell yourself that you get anxious. Remember that once you apply a label, that behaviour is perpetuated into the future. You create a self-fulfilling prophecy that says you will get anxious.

Once that label has been applied, you will find yourself getting anxious any time you are faced with a situation that makes you uncomfortable. Anxiety becomes a vicious cycle.

Whew! What a marathon effort!

Before we go on to consider how you might overcome your anxiety, take a moment to reflect on the old Sun Tzu quote I put at the beginning of this section. He said that it is important to know both yourself and your enemy. I want you to think of anxiety as your enemy.

In the 6th century BC, Sun Tzu said if you know your enemy you can defeat them. If you think of anxiety as an entity separate to you – a sneaky, nasty, and often overwhelming enemy – it's easier to consider annihilating it!

Remember to take some time to stop and reflect on what I've said so far in this chapter before we move on with strategies to combat anxiety. Once you are sure you understand how anxiety operates, how the enemy works, you are ready to plan your attack!

So how can you overcome anxiety?

To a large extent, overcoming anxiety is simply a matter of:

a) breaking the cycle

b) losing the label.

As I said, anxiety is a sneaky critter. I say sneaky critter because it's as though it becomes a thing you blame when you avoid situations and stop doing life stuff. If you think of anxiety as an innate part of you, then it's harder to get rid of the label: That's just the way I am. I've always been anxious.

If you think of anxiety as something outside of you, as just another bad habit you've developed that can be rewritten, then you can start to plan and problem-solve how to change that particular habit. Let's start by looking at how you can use the information I've given you to break the anxiety cycle.

Breaking the Anxiety Cycle

If you look at the three different boxes outlined in the anxiety cycle diagram, it will become clear how you can use that information to break the cycle. You can break the cycle by changing your physical reaction, your thought patterns, and/or your behavioural response. Any break in the cycle is going to stop the cycle in its tracks. When you break the anxiety cycle you will feel more in control and less anxious.

Changing Your Physical Reaction
Thinking back to the information I gave you in Chapter Two, you will remember that when we feel threatened our autonomic nervous system shifts into fight or flight mode or distress mode. When you shift into distress mode there

What If?

is a series of physical changes that occur. Specifically, your body is preparing to get you out of a dangerous situation.

These changes are highly adaptive when you are indeed in a life-threatening situation. They are not so helpful when you are sitting at home contemplating a trip to the shops. If you allow your body to stay in this heightened state while there is no danger present, your mind will search for the cause of the distress. If you are reacting to the idea of a trip to the shops, then your mind will perceive that as a dangerous situation and will automatically generate negative thoughts around that situation, and thus the cycle is maintained.

To stop the cycle at the physical reaction, it is necessary to shift from distress mode to relax mode. You already know an incredibly effective technique to trigger this shift. Yes, that's right. You simply start breathing through your eyes. The sooner you do this when you notice yourself being triggered, the easier the shift will be. Refer back to Chapter Two if you need to refresh your knowledge of this technique.

Breathing Through Your Eyes. When you successfully shift to breathing through your eyes, you will notice your body start to relax and you will immediately feel calmer. At this point your body is in relax mode. You are able to switch on your thinking brain and problem-solve the matter at hand. The anxiety cycle has been broken because you are no longer feeling distressed, no longer feeling physically anxious.

Breathing through your eyes is a technique that not only triggers the shift into relax mode, it also grounds you in the present moment.

Grounding Techniques. There are many grounding techniques that you might use in conjunction with the breathing exercise. Anything that gets you to focus your attention on something other than your spiralling thoughts and sense of physical distress can be used to ground you in the moment.

Grounding techniques have their roots in mindfulness. When you focus your attention on a particular aspect of your body, for example, you are in essence reminding yourself to be present in the moment. We will discuss mindfulness in more detail in Chapter Eight when we cover stress.

Some ideas for grounding techniques include:

- pushing your feet into the floor, noticing that the floor seems to push back even harder
- stretching your muscles
- stroking your palm
- taking a sip of water
- pushing your palms together in front of you
- tapping your foot to music.

There are obviously many more grounding techniques. Once again, I have provided some ideas, but what works for you is for you to decide. Really, anything can be grounding if it brings your attention away from your thoughts and back into the present moment. These techniques take you out of the spiralling cycle. They allow you to slow down, encourage you to let go of the negative thoughts and recognise that

What If?

you can take control of your own physical actions in spite of the distress.

Now, let's consider what to do to change those pesky thought patterns.

Changing Your Thought Patterns
You already know how to step away from sabotage through language. In Chapter Four, you have access to the four main types of sabotage and techniques to reframe them. Here, I will simply explain how the sabotage works to exacerbate your anxious thoughts.

I've already mentioned that if you think of yourself as anxious, then you will behave as such. This is known as labelling.

Labelling. You effectively label yourself and your behaviour and perpetuate the behaviour into the future. When you label yourself as anxious you automatically tend to name every feeling of discomfort as anxiety. You are also hypervigilant to your anxiety response, and no matter how quickly and effectively you shut down that anxiety response, you will give more weight to the brief anxious reaction than to how effectively and quickly you take control and step away from the anxiety. I see this pattern again and again. No matter how effectively my clients learn to master their anxiety, while they are still labelling themselves as anxious, they continue to notice and highlight moments of anxiety. It is a constant battle because they are not attending to the most important aspect of the situation which is how well they manage the situation once they apply the strategy.

Once you are effectively using the strategies to stop the language sabotage and calm your physical system, recognise that anxiety is no longer an issue for you. You have mastered it! Accept it, and when you catch yourself labelling yourself as anxious, put the label into the past where it belongs. Try saying to yourself, "I used to get anxious, but now I am in control of my reactions".

Another way in which we use labelling when it comes to anxiety is to label any level of discomfort in relation to an upcoming situation as anxiety. Please remember, you can feel out of your comfort zone in any situation until you are used to it. You may be out of your comfort zone the first day on your new job but not after your first week.

There are some situations, however, in which you may always feel a little uncomfortable. Let's use a job interview as an example. Most people are out of their comfort zone in a job interview. A job interview has a significant degree of pressure attached to it. You want to perform well enough to be offered the job. So, if you feel out of your comfort zone in such a situation, is your discomfort perfectly normal or is it an anxious response?

Here's a rule of thumb to apply. If it is normal for people to feel uncomfortable in that situation, you are out of your comfort zone. It is important to realise that:

- if you label yourself as anxious in this situation, you are mislabelling.
- it is okay to be uncomfortable.
- managing uncomfortable situations can often lead to personal growth.

What If?

So, before labelling your reaction to a situation, think about whether it would be a normal response to be uncomfortable in that situation, or whether you are responding to an imagined threat as you do when you feel anxious. If you recognise that it's normal to be uncomfortable in the situation then do not label it as anxiety. Once you learn that lesson you will likely find that your anxiety diminishes rapidly.

All or Nothing Thinking. You may find yourself exploring a lot of what ifs when you ruminate about the future, remembering that anxiety is the anticipation of a negative event or outcome. The what ifs tend to lead to predictions of your inability to cope with the situation. In this case, all or nothing thinking is likely to be one of your self-limiting patterns.

When you succumb to all or nothing thinking you are basically telling yourself the situation is impossible to deal with. When you are facing an anxiety-provoking situation you probably tell yourself stories about the situation that lead you to the belief that you cannot cope in that situation. That sense of I can't leads to a typical behavioural reaction of avoidance. I can't cope with the situation so I will avoid the situation. It makes perfect sense. Well, it would make perfect sense if you are correct in your assumption that you can't cope with the situation.

Let's assume that you can in fact cope with the anxiety-provoking situation. It is not necessary to tell yourself that it will be easy. That would likely be a step too far. It might well be a struggle, but with planning and a little courage you can get through the situation without panicking. How good would that feel? Simply by shifting your language to the possible you stop it from being impossible. Once it's no longer impossible, it's just a matter of making a plan and following through.

Now I'm going to talk about the last form of language sabotage I think really impacts anxiety levels.

Blaming. Blaming and anxiety. What is the connection, you ask? Well, as I see it, when we feel anxious about a situation, we tend to blame the situation for making us feel anxious. "Public speaking makes me so anxious. I just know I'll stuff up and make a fool of myself."

When you catch yourself blaming a situation for your reactive response, you are telling yourself that you do not have control in the situation. You are effectively telling yourself that the situation is in control, as bizarre as that might seem. The situation causes you to respond in this manner.

The solution, of course, is simple. I allowed myself to react that way in the past. Now, however, I have tools and strategies to manage my anxiety. In fact, I have the tools and strategies at hand to stop feeling anxious altogether. I know how to relax by breathing through my eyes. I can stop sabotaging myself through my language. I have the capacity to plan and problem-solve any situation that arises. I can cope. I do not have to run away from the situation. I can cope even if I don't like it much. I can cope. It may not be comfortable or easy, but it will get easier as I build confidence. I can do this.

What If?

Now let's explore what you can do instead of running away and avoiding a situation that traditionally causes you anxiety.

Changing Your Behavioural Response
The main behavioural reaction to an anxiety-provoking situation is avoidance. Avoidance often means not putting yourself in the situation at all, but sometimes it's not quite that clear cut. Imagine you feel quite anxious at the idea of going to the supermarket. You might get diarrhoea when you get anxious. Getting ready to go out takes time because you end up racing to the toilet a few times in the 30 minutes before you are due to set out. This leads you to a fear that you may have an accident while shopping. This has never actually happened, but you have formed a habit now of only going to shops where you know exactly where the toilets are located. You also choose to go early in the morning or later at night when there are fewer people around because you'll get in and out more quickly. The last thing you do to prepare is limit your shop to as few items as possible. You figure you can get in and out in under 20 minutes. You arrive in the car park, take a deep breath and then race around doing your grocery shop. You get back to the car and breathe again. Okay, I know you do breathe while in the shop, but I guarantee your breathing is fast and shallow. You would never consider wandering around the complex to window shop. You race in and out at the speed of light. Racing in and out of a situation will only exacerbate your anxiety. It won't resolve it. It somehow provides further proof that the situation is bad and you can't cope. This response helps that big red balloon get so very big!

In this situation, while you have a plan of attack, you are not really feeling in control. You are avoiding crowds, queues, long shopping lists, etc. I've had clients who have literally abandoned their shopping and raced back to the car because suddenly they felt unable to cope. Unfortunately, the high levels of distress do not resolve when you approach the situation in this fashion. In fact, you are effectively confirming that the situation is highly stressful and anxiety-provoking because you do not give yourself the opportunity to discover that it's actually safe and you can in fact go shopping the same way that a non-anxious person does.

If you were to create a plan to change your behaviour, what might that look like? You will calm your physical system by breathing through your eyes. You will reframe your sabotaging thoughts and remind yourself that you are able to cope in the situation. You will plan how to respond if you start to feel uncomfortable utilising the same strategies.

In other words, you choose to be proactive and in control of your behavioural response rather than reactive to the fear.

IN SUMMARY

1. Anxiety is an irrational response to an imagined threat. It feels real, but often anxiety is simply fear of the fear.

2. Anxiety is a cycle. By breaking the cycle you reduce or eliminate your anxiety.

3. The anxiety cycle can be broken by:

    a. calming your body and shifting into relax mode

    b. reframing your language to eliminate sabotage through language

    c. being proactive rather than reactive and choosing to deal with a situation rather than avoiding it.

4. Stop labelling yourself as anxious. When you successfully use the strategies, you no longer need to think of yourself as anxious.

5. Remember that everyone will face situations in their lives that put them outside their comfort zones. If you are in a situation that is outside your comfort zone, it is a normal human response to feel uncomfortable. That is not the same as feeling anxious.

6. If you are struggling to break the anxiety cycle using the techniques taught in this chapter and in Section One of this book, consider seeking professional help.

CHAPTER EIGHT

Too Many Boxes!

Stress. Stress is part of life. I have stress in my life. You have stress in your life. But what is stress, you ask? And why do you sometimes feel stressed and at other times you feel as though you are coping?

These are good questions. Let me start by painting a word picture for you.

Think of the stressors in your life as a single pile of boxes, all higgledy-piggledy over in the corner of the room. Big boxes, small boxes, wide boxes, skinny boxes, piled randomly one on top of the other. Big boxes are on small boxes, small boxes on big boxes. This pile of boxes has not been planned. It simply grew as different stressors turned up and landed on the pile!

So, stress and stressor, what do these words mean? How are they different?

For the sake of clarity in this chapter, I'm going to use the terms to mean slightly different things. A stressor is the individual item or situation that is causing you stress. A stressor can be seen as a burden, a chore, a responsibility, a task that must be completed, a big event, or just pressure to perform. In other words, each box on your pile represents a stressor.

Stress is your physical, emotional, mental, and/or psychological response to the pressures of life and the burdens that you take on. Feeling stressed is like carrying a heavy weight on your shoulders. You may even have said that you carry your stress in your shoulders and neck. Thus, when you feel stressed you are reacting to the pressures of life. Many of these pressures or stressors are external to you.

Stress sneaks up on you one stressor at a time. The problem with your stress response is that it is cumulative, which simply means that as another stressor is added to the pile your overall experience of feeling stressed increases. What you end up responding to is not just the latest stressor, but the combined impact of all the stressors that are in your pile of boxes. Unfortunately, that last stressor may well prove to be the straw that broke the camel's back.

Stressors come in all shapes and sizes and involve many aspects of your life. Stressors might include the expectations you believe other people have of you, expectations you might have of yourself, whether you'll get the response you want from your latest social media post, financial responsibilities, and so on. Some potentially quite exciting times in your life can also contribute to the stress you feel at different times in your life. Getting married, buying a house, starting a new job, or even just doing something for the first time may contribute to your overall feelings of stress. Other less exciting but certainly stressful events that you may face in your lifetime include the death of a loved one, death of a pet, personal injury, family emergencies, relationship breakdowns. The list goes on.

Even prehistoric humans had stressors in their lives, such as finding enough food, finding shelter, risk of injury or illness, death in their circle, maybe even keeping the fire alive. The stressors they faced were significant, but they had nowhere near the same number of stressors you likely face in your day-to-day life.

So how many stressors can you cope with? At what point do you tip over the edge into feeling stressed? How does stress affect you?

How Does Stress Affect You?

The stress response, like anxiety, triggers a shift from relax mode to distress mode. Even a relatively small stress response might increase your heart rate, quicken your breathing, and raise your blood pressure. Chronic, high levels of stress may affect your immune system so that you tend to catch whatever is going around. In some extreme cases, stress can lead to a stroke or heart attack.

So, stress is not your friend. Stress is, in fact, another example of the enemy.

How Do You Know When You Are Stressed?

Are you stressed? Well, there are plenty of cues for you to notice when you look for them. Let's consider cues that relate to your body, your brain and your behaviour.

Body (Physical Symptoms)
- Tension in neck and shoulders
- Reflux and/or indigestion
- Clenching in the gut
- Tightness in the chest
- Shallow breathing
- High blood pressure
- Elevated heart rate
- Diarrhoea and/or constipation
- Headache
- Poor sleep
- Fatigue
- Getting sick frequently

Too Many Boxes!

Brain (Thoughts and Brain Function)
- Racing thoughts
- Difficulty letting go of racing thoughts
- Pressure language (I have to, I've got to, etc.)
- All or nothing language
- Poor concentration
- Feeling mentally overwhelmed

Behaviour (Reactive Response)
- Snappiness
- Irritability
- Impatience
- Intolerance
- Over-reacting to situations
- Agitation
- Angry outbursts
- Impulsivity
- Rushing to get things done without prior planning
- Distractibility
- Difficulty relaxing

Your observing self, the part that can sit back and take notice of what you are feeling and how you are responding, is able to pinpoint the signs of stress when primed to do so.

It's easy to recognise that you are stressed when your pile of boxes suddenly reaches critical mass and you explode. It takes more refined skill to recognise you are stressed before you are set to explode.

You might notice tension in your shoulders and neck, or a change in the way your digestive system is working. You may recognise that you are having to be super organised to get through the tasks you have scheduled. You might notice yourself snapping at the kids or getting irritated with a slow co-worker. You might find yourself dreaming about work and waking up in the middle of the night creating lists of things to be done. There are so many different cues that can indicate that you are stressed, that the pressure is building.

Try gently moving your head down to one side so that your right ear is moving towards your right shoulder. How does that feel? Can you feel tightness in your neck? If you can, it's a sure sign you are carrying stress in your body.

If you imagine the pile of boxes I mentioned earlier, it is obvious that the higher the pile the higher your level of stress. If the pile of boxes only comes to your waist, you are likely to feel relatively relaxed. If the pile of boxes is up to your chest, you will be feeling the pressure even though you are coping by being relatively organised. If the pile of boxes is up around the level of your head you will be feeling quite stressed. You might even feel as though you are struggling to breathe. At this point, the stress feels overwhelming. You may well feel that you are struggling to cope with all the burdens and pressures resting on your shoulders.

The sooner you realise that your pile of boxes is growing, the better. When you monitor your stress response you can also be proactive about managing it. Your observing self and thinking brain working together will give you the best outcome.

Dealing with Your Pile of Boxes

It's interesting that when your pile of boxes gets to around chest height or higher there is a tendency for you to be less efficient at managing your stressors. At this point you may well let small, easily managed stressors just land and sit on the pile, thereby increasing the pile even further.

One strategy to consider when you start to feel your stressors mounting up is to imagine separating your pile of boxes into two piles.

The first pile contains only the stressors that you can resolve immediately and relatively easily. Examples might include paying a bill, getting your Christmas shopping out of the way, getting an assignment or report finished, or making an appointment with the dentist. There can be lots of little things that add to your pile of stress when you don't get in and deal with them. Often the longer you put off dealing with a stressor, the more that stressor tends to grow. The box effectively expands and gets taller. If you leave your Christmas shopping till the last minute, it tends to be much more stressful than if you get it out of the way earlier.

The second pile contains those stressors that can't simply be resolved. Examples might include your mortgage or rent, other financial pressures, work stresses, relationship issues, and so on. These individual boxes of stress can be made bigger or smaller by how you respond to them.

If you feel in control of your own actions and reactions around a particular box of stress, then the box still contains stress, but it is smaller than if you do not feel in control of your response. For example, if you have a mortgage, and organise to regularly pay more into the mortgage than the minimum requirement, you feel proactive. You are working towards reducing the mortgage repayments as quickly as possible and creating a buffer for yourself if your situation changes down the track. Your mortgage box is still likely to be there for many years, but the amount of stress associated with it is far less than for the person who just manages to scrape together the bare minimum repayment each month.

So ultimately it is you being proactive and taking control of your own actions and reactions that allows you to actively reduce your stress response.

There might well be times, however, when you will knowingly, willingly, and deliberately increase your stress levels beyond the point where it is comfortable for you. This might involve taking on a short-term project over and above your regular job or setting a strict and imminent deadline for a project the completion of which pushes you out of your comfort zone. The one piece of advice I would give is that if you are knowingly taking on more stress than is comfortable, set yourself a relatively short period for which you are committing to such a stressful regime. High levels of stress on a long-term basis can significantly impact on your health.

Now let us consider some other strategies for reducing our experience of stress in general. Some helpful lifestyle choices that can lower your overall stress levels include exercise, a healthy diet, and a good night's sleep on a regular basis. Social connections can also help us destress.

Now that you are aware of your pile of boxes, let's drill down and consider the impact those boxes have on you. Let's start by considering the impact of stress on the body and what you can do about it.

Stress in the Body

To reduce stress in your body, you first need to be aware that it exists. We have previously talked about your observing self, the part of you that notices how you are feeling and what's going on around you. To make a good plan, you need information. Your observing self is your information gatherer.

Scanning your body is a relatively quick and easy way to assess your levels of tension. It takes a little practice, but once you have the technique in place, you will find it extremely useful to gauge how your body is responding in any given situation. Your body's response will often provide your first clue that you are feeling stressed.

Scanning your body is often one of the first steps in a mindfulness process. I will cover mindfulness in more detail a little later in this chapter, but for now I will just say that being mindful simply means being fully present in the moment.

Scan Your Body
I suggest you begin by getting yourself comfortable, sitting or lying down, and close your eyes. Continue breathing normally and let your attention move either up or down your body. Notice whether there is tension in your neck and shoulders. Is your breathing fast or slow? Look for any sense of discomfort in your chest and/or stomach. Does your forehead feel tight or relaxed? Do you have a headache? Are you suffering with reflux or indigestion? Remember you are just observing, noticing how you are feeling. If your thoughts intrude, acknowledge them then let them go as you return to scanning your body.

As you get more used to noticing how your body is feeling, you will likely be able to do a quick scan standing up with your eyes open. Until you get very used to scanning your body without getting distracted by your thoughts or your other senses, I suggest you perform the body scan with your eyes closed, and ideally sitting or lying down to keep yourself safe.

Once you have scanned your body, you can make a plan for dealing with whatever level of stress you find in your body. If your body is completely relaxed, congratulations! If you have found stress, then consider the cause of the stress and plan to deal with it proactively.

Too Many Boxes!

To physically reduce stress in your body, the first technique I will remind you of is to breathe through your eyes. I introduced and explained the concept of breathing through your eyes fully in Chapter Two should you need to refresh your memory of the process.

Breathe Through Your Eyes
Take a few breaths into your eyes then rescan your body to check for residual tension. This may be all you need to do to reset your body to relax mode. If not, you may benefit from exploring mindfulness or some other form of meditation.

Mindfulness
Mindfulness is simply the act of being fully present in the moment. It involves learning to engage our observing selves and let our thoughts go. Our chatty minds tend to take us away from the present into either the past or the future. Learning to be fully present in the moment is a useful technique that seems to slow the world down long enough for you to reset and regroup. Mindfulness is also about appreciating the moment. Remind yourself to stop and smell the roses, as the old saying goes.

You can perform any activity in a mindful fashion: you can eat mindfully, walk mindfully, brush your teeth mindfully. Mindfulness exercises often get you to explore each of your senses in turn. Stopping your mind from interfering is good practice for any mindfulness technique. There are plenty of mindfulness apps available online if you want to be guided through a process. Otherwise, you can use the principles I have outlined here to learn to be mindful wherever you are. This is a simple exercise that focuses on one sense at a time.

You can run through the whole process or do an abbreviated version depending on the time you have available.

Spend as much or as little time as you like on each of the senses. Remember to simply observe and notice. If your mind starts telling you stories or analysing what you are experiencing in the moment, simply acknowledge the interruption, then refocus your attention back to your senses.

To start:

- Take a deep breath into your eyes.
- Continue to breathe deeply, focusing your attention on your breath. Notice the sensation of the breath.
- When you are ready, shift your attention to the rest of your body. Scan your body from top to bottom.
- Notice any areas of tension and imagine breathing into those areas, one at a time. Allow those areas to let go and relax as you breathe into them.
- Notice your sense of touch. As you scan your body notice the sensation of your feet on the floor, the clothes touching your skin. Gently run the finger of one hand over the back of your other hand. Notice the sensations of both the finger and the hand. Play a little with your sense of touch. Observe the sensations.
- When you are ready, shift your focus to your sense of hearing. Notice what you can hear, ignoring your other senses in the process.

- Next, shift your focus to your sense of smell. Notice what you can smell, ignoring your other senses in the process.

- When ready, shift your focus to your sense of sight. Notice what you can see, ignoring your other senses in the process.

- Next, shift your focus back to your breath. Notice that while you have been focusing on other aspects of your experience, your body has continued to breathe.

- Finally, return your attention to the room or whatever space you are in.

For a shorter mindfulness exercise to help you quickly reset and regroup simply focus on your breath:

- Take a deep breath into your eyes.

- Continue to breathe deeply, focusing your attention on your breath. Notice the sensation of the breath.

- If a thought intrudes, simply notice the thought, then let it go and return your attention to your breath.

- When you are ready, return your attention to whatever situation you are dealing with.

An excellent time to practise mindfulness is when you are eating. Stress plays havoc with your digestive system so eating mindfully is a fabulous way to limit the physical impact that stress can have.

Mindfulness while eating has some excellent side benefits, including slowing you down, increasing your enjoyment of the meal, and allowing you to notice when you have eaten enough. I suggest before starting your meal that you sit and breathe through your eyes for at least two breaths to relax your body so that your digestive system is working in optimal mode. When you start to eat, be mindful of the look, smell, texture and taste of the food. Take time to enjoy your meal.

Notice, also, how your body is responding to the meal. Notice your sense of hunger at the beginning of the meal. Notice whether you salivate when you smell and see the meal. How does your body respond to the first mouthful? Notice how your body feels as you move through the meal. Take note when you start to feel as though you are no longer hungry. When you recognise that you are no longer hungry, stop eating. Stop eating even if that means leaving food on your plate.

If, after completing the breathing and mindfulness exercises, you are still noticing significant levels of physical tension in your body, a different type of physical intervention may be required. The following exercise is called progressive muscle relaxation.

Progressive Muscle Relaxation
Progressive muscle relaxation teaches you how to relax your muscles in a simple two-step process that helps you both learn to relax your muscles at will while also learning to recognise the presence of physical tension in the first place. Simply put, you first clench your muscles then relax them. By observing the difference, you are also learning to recognise the physical presence of muscular tension more

readily. There are various scripts freely available on the internet. You may well find one that provides a recording which steps you through the process. In this chapter, I will use a standard script that is easy to follow.

Through this exercise you will focus your attention on discrete areas of the body, tensing and relaxing as you go. I like to start with the feet and work up to your head, but feel free to complete the process in the reverse order if that works better for you. The reason I choose to work up the body is simply that most people carry their tension largely in their shoulders and necks. By starting at the feet and working up, you are giving your body lots of practice in tensing and relaxing before you get to the most affected areas of your body. It makes sense to me that the body learns through practice. You may find it easier to relax your neck and shoulders if you have relaxed virtually your whole body before you get to them.

When you are working on the legs and arms do one side of the body at a time. Notice the sensations in each targeted muscle group through each part of the process. It's important to notice the difference between the sensations when you tense and relax your muscles. When you are starting with one side of the body, you can also compare your newly relaxed side with the side you have yet to put through the process.

To start the process, you ideally want to be in a quiet place that has no distractions. Wear loose comfortable clothing. Make yourself comfortable either lying down or sitting in a comfortable chair.

The process:

1. Breathe through your eyes two or three times, allowing yourself to relax as much as possible.

2. Focus on the muscle group you are targeting, for example, the right foot.

3. Take a deep breath in through your nose and hold for up to five seconds as you tense your target muscle group as hard as you comfortably can. Be careful not to tense so hard you hurt yourself.

4. Exhale through your mouth as you relax the target muscle group. Spend around 10 to 15 seconds noticing how your relaxed muscles feel.

5. Repeat steps 2 to 4 until you get through all the different muscle groups.

The different muscle groups:

1. Legs (do one complete leg, then repeat with the other leg)

    a. Foot: Curl your toes downwards.

    b. Lower leg and foot: Tighten your calf muscles by pulling your toes up towards you.

    c. Whole leg: Squeeze your thigh muscles while tightening your calf muscles by pulling your toes up towards you.

2. Arms (do one complete arm, then repeat with the other arm)

    a. Hand: Clench your fist.

    b. Whole arm: Draw your forearm up towards your shoulder to tighten your biceps and show off your muscles while clenching your fist.

3. Buttocks: Clench your buttocks.

4. Stomach: Suck your stomach in.

5. Chest: Breath in deeply while pulling your stomach in.

6. Neck: Be careful as you tense these muscles. Remember tension often settles into the neck. Facing forward, tip your head back slowly as though you are looking up to the ceiling.

7. Shoulders: Be careful as you tense these muscles. Remember tension often settles into the shoulders. Tense your shoulder muscles as you lift both shoulders up towards your ears.

8. Mouth: Open your mouth as wide as you can.

9. Eyes: Squeeze your eyes tightly shut.

10. Forehead: Raise your eyebrows as far as you can.

With that exercise, I have finished talking about the physical aspects of stress and tension. Let's now look at your thoughts and behaviours which can be discussed together.

Stepping into Adult Mode

When you feel stressed you may well find yourself acting like a bratty three-year-old. Behavioural symptoms of stress often include snappiness, anger, impatience, intolerance, over-reaction, impulsivity, and so on. Bratty three-year-old territory at its best. Additionally, the more stressed you feel, the more disorganised you are likely to become as the pressures facing you become overwhelming.

Your thoughts, when stressed, are often unhelpful and self-limiting. You may well add to the pressures you are facing by sabotaging yourself with your thoughts and language. When you start to feel the pressure build, set your observing self the task of identifying what negative language you are using. When you identify all or nothing thinking, labelling, pressure language or blaming, simply go back to Chapter Four and review the strategies, then practise, practise, practise.

Also, going back to basics, when you notice yourself feeling stressed, stop and breathe through your eyes. Chapter Two covers that technique. Use that moment of space and time you create around you to get your thinking brain onto the problem at hand. Once you have your thinking brain in gear, review your priorities, problem-solve and make your plans.

Prioritising
Prioritising is a skill like any other. It might help to write down all the commitments you are dealing with, and then work out the relative level of importance versus urgency for each of them. Imagine plotting a graph with importance on the X axis and urgency on the Y axis, as shown.

Too Many Boxes!

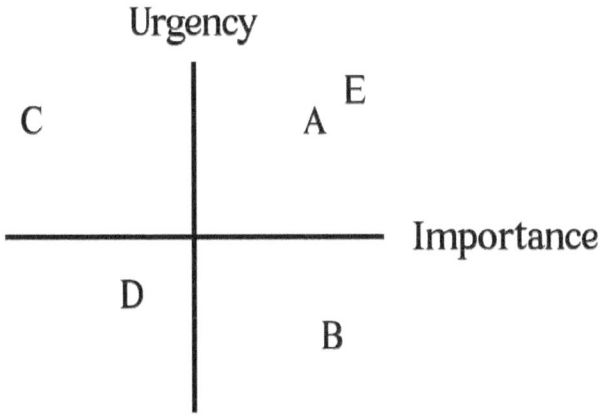

Let us consider the five items I have graphed.

- Item A is both of high urgency and high importance, for example:
    - The job application you have been working on for the past week must be in by 5pm today.
- Item B is of low urgency but high importance, for example:
    - It's your 20th wedding anniversary in two weeks and you haven't bought a gift.
- Item C is of high urgency but low importance, for example:
    - An old school friend you haven't seen for a month is leaving town tomorrow and you would like to catch up before they go.
- Item D is of low urgency and low importance, for example:

- You noticed yesterday your car seat cover is getting a little worn around the edges. You want to look for a new set of seat covers.
- Item E is both of high urgency and high importance, for example:
    - Your electricity bill is overdue. If you don't pay it by 5pm today, they have threatened to cut your electricity off.

If these are the five commitments you are juggling, then your priorities become clear with this exercise. In this case both Item A, the job application, and Item E, the electricity bill, are urgent and important. Both are a priority and thus compete for your available time.

You consider which task to complete first. You realise that if you focus on the job application first you may run out of time to pay the bill before the deadline. Alternatively, you can quickly pay the bill and then get to work on finishing the job application, completing both tasks by the deadline of 5pm. Item E, paying the bill, thus becomes your first priority as it can be quickly finalised, followed by Item A, the job application.

Item B, buying an anniversary present, while highly important does not have the same degree of urgency as the date is still two weeks away. It can wait until you have more time to attend to it.

Item C, catching up with your friend before they leave town, is urgent in that they won't be here after tomorrow, but perhaps not so important as you did see them a month ago and you are no longer such close friends.

Item D, replacing the seat covers, can wait until it's convenient. It's neither urgent nor overly important.

By compiling a to-do list and prioritising the relative urgency and importance of items on the list, it becomes clearer which items should be tackled in what order. It also helps you to set achievable deadlines as you work out how long to spend on each task.

IN SUMMARY

A degree of stress is a normal experience for humans in this complex world we live in. You have a unique pile of stressors that adds to your experience of stress.

As your stress level builds you can recognise it by taking notice of your:

- physical symptoms, including muscular tension and digestive issues

- self-limiting thoughts and sabotage through language, particularly pressure language and all or nothing language

- behavioural over-reaction such as snappiness, irritability, intolerance, and impulsivity.

When you recognise that your stress levels are building up it is important that you manage your current stressors proactively to limit the stress before it becomes debilitating. You can help manage stress through:

- separating your pile of boxes and prioritising stressors that can be finalised

- breathing through your eyes to reset your body to relax mode

- being proactive in reducing sabotage through language and self-limiting thoughts

- practising mindfulness

- using progressive muscle relaxation
- using your thinking brain to be proactive in dealing with the tasks at hand
- prioritising tasks effectively.

CHAPTER NINE

The Swamp Monster

Depression is an enemy that sneaks up on you. Winston Churchill famously referred to his depressive symptoms as the black dog. It's a term you are familiar with. The black dog of depression, the dog that creeps up on you and leads you on a downward spiral. The aspect I like about the black dog metaphor is that you are looking at depression as something outside of yourself. The aspect I don't like about the black dog metaphor is simply that I like dogs, and I personally think a dog in your life promotes good health rather than depression.

You might think of depression as a parasite, sucking the life out of you. I always picture depression as Gollum from J. R. R. Tolkien's incredible novels, The Hobbit and The

Get it Together Forever

Lord of the Rings. I paint a picture for my clients of Gollum clinging to their backs, his arms wrapped strongly around their necks as he sucks their energy from them.

Another image I quite like is that of an ugly green monster that drags you into the swamp to keep it company. The swamp is full of sticky, smelly mud which makes it difficult for you to drag yourself out. Every time you try to get out the monster pulls you back. To get out, you must fight the monster off as you drag yourself out of the swamp.

Beating depression can be hard work. I won't lie to you. It takes effort. It's not simply a matter of telling yourself to get over it. You must be prepared to put up a fight. The effort is worth it, though. When you fight to get out of the swamp of doom and you succeed, you are unlikely to let yourself dive back in. Depression is an enemy that you can fight. If you are prepared to fight and able to fight, then depression is an enemy you can beat!

As Sun Tzu would say in The Art of War, to win the fight you must know yourself and your enemy. It's important not to mix the two up. You are not your enemy.

In the first two sections of this book you learned a lot about yourself. I trust that you have taken the lessons on board and have started to appreciate and respect yourself. In this chapter, I will teach you more about the enemy, depression, and how to beat it.

One of the first and most important lessons I want you to take on board is that the depression you feel is not you! You

The Swamp Monster

are not your depression. If you put the label on yourself and call yourself depressed, you create the reality of being depressed. It's as though you claim the depression as your own, and in effect, you give it control over you.

It can be very difficult to shift away from being the person you tell yourself you are. The nature of self-limiting beliefs is to put limits on you. This is one of the reasons that the stories we take on as children are often so difficult to get rid of. It's not that you cannot change your story and choose a different path, it's that you tend to cement the story in place by telling yourself, "That's just who I am". Those old stories tend to define the labels and limits we attach to ourselves.

If you can picture depression as a monstrous being that is separate from you, a parasite that you have allowed to live off your energy, then it's easier to make the choice to fight it. Fight the enemy. It is not difficult to think of depression as the enemy. Think of a monster for whom you are food. I think of Gollum or the swamp monster, but if those images don't resonate with you, perhaps you might picture depression as a big hairy spider. Depression is like a huge spider that has crept up on you, injected you with a paralysing drug, and stuck you in a web for safe keeping.

Think about it. How do you feel when you are depressed? Your energy levels are low, you struggle to be bothered with anything, you withdraw socially, your appetite and sleep are affected, even getting out of bed and getting dressed can be a struggle. Your thoughts tend to be full of all or nothing thinking and labelling. You are probably adding pressure language to the mix telling yourself you should do this or you have to do that, then struggling to find the motivation to actually do anything. The spider is whispering in your ear telling you that you can't be bothered, it's all too hard. You could think of this as a type of paralysis if you hold your mouth the right way and squint a little. As a metaphor, I think the big hairy spider works quite nicely. Choose one of my images or create your own depression monster. Don't make it pretty. Depression is not pretty. Depression sucks the energy out of the room. Depression is doom and gloom.

The big issue with dealing with depression is the lack of energy and interest you feel as a result. To make matters worse, you tend to stop doing all the helpful things that can fight depression, such as exercise, a good diet, getting Vitamin D from the sun, catching up with friends and family, listening to music, and keeping up your hobbies and interests. You are more likely to find yourself spending the day in front of the television in your pyjamas unless you have to get up and go to work or school or wherever.

Obviously recognising you are depressed is probably not a huge issue. You are very aware of it. The question remains, though, how do you fight something that starts by taking away your interest in fighting?

Good question! And yes, I do have some ideas about how to go about it.

Dealing with Depression

Psychologists often talk about a technique called behavioural activation when it comes to shifting depression. Behavioural activation is a jargonistic term that in one sense simply means, "Start moving to keep moving". Once you start doing something proactive, it's easier to keep the momentum building.

Behavioural activation works on principles I covered in Section One of this book. I highlighted the fact that while your emotional state can influence your thoughts and your behaviours, the relationships between those three elements run both ways. Certainly, if you are feeling depressed (emotion) you have a tendency to stop doing activities you otherwise enjoy (behaviour) and your language (thoughts) tends to be negative. Now ask yourself what might be the impact on your emotional response if you were to get up in the morning and go for a walk? What might be the impact on your emotional response if you put some nice music on as you make yourself a tasty and healthy breakfast? How might your emotional response change if you were to shift your language from "I can't do that" to "It's difficult for me, but I can make a plan and try to get it done"?

When you change your thoughts and/or change the way you respond to a situation, your emotional reaction will change accordingly. When you are feeling depressed you do not feel in control of your actions and reactions. You grind to a halt. When you tell yourself the situation is not impossible and you force yourself to start moving again, your momentum tends to pick up. I invite you to channel

Thomas the Tank Engine for a moment, "I think I can . . . I think I can . . . I think I can . . . I know I can!" Thanks to Reverend Wilbert Awdry and his son, Christopher Awdry, for bringing Thomas to life!

While you are still smiling, as I hope channelling Thomas did indeed put a smile on your face, let us consider some of the simple things you can do to start feeling less depressed.

Exercise
You know that you feel better when you exercise. Exercise doesn't have to be a formal routine. Going for a walk is exercise. Working in your garden, cleaning the bathroom, playing outside with the kids, or dancing to the song you are listening to are all forms of exercise.

Planning to start your day by going for a walk is a good way to include exercise in your daily routine. I would suggest you get your clothes and shoes ready the night before so that in the morning you get straight into your walking gear. Then get out and walk for a minimum of ten minutes. Whether you walk to the shop for a coffee, walk on the beach or through a park, or walk the neighbourhood is up to you. Aim to build up to at least 30 minutes of walking in a session. More is fine, but please set yourself goals you know you can achieve to start with. That opens the door for another old saying, "Don't try to run before you can walk".

Company while walking can also be beneficial to your mood. Walk with your family or a friend. Take the dog for a walk.

Current recommendations are that you aim to take a minimum of 30 minutes of moderate intensity exercise most days of the week. Depending on your current level of fitness you may plan to work up to this level. Remember that as you increase your level of exercise you will increase your level of fitness. An increased level of fitness will make you feel better physically and mentally. Regular exercise is also associated with better sleep patterns and increased energy levels, so by exercising regularly you increase your physical capacity to do more. Regular exercise has also been associated with a reduction of negative thoughts.

Remember that the hardest part of changing a pattern of behaviour is starting the new behaviour. Once you make a start, it's easier to continue, so take a deep breath and get up and start moving. When you are trying to develop a new pattern, consistency is the key. I would suggest that you decide on a particular form of convenient exercise (such as walking) and plan to do that at least four to five times a week. More is great but start by setting yourself goals you feel comfortable reaching.

Another idea is to spend some time practising mindfulness while exercising. Notice how you are feeling, notice the world around you, notice the bird song, notice the sun on your skin, notice pretty gardens, and so on.

Caution. If you have chronic or acute medical conditions which impact on your ability to exercise, please speak with your treating practitioner before planning your new exercise program.

Vitamin D (the Sunshine Vitamin)
While the evidence is still being debated as to whether Vitamin D supplements help lift depression per se, there is no doubt that spending time outdoors with sunshine and fresh air is good for your emotional state. It is common in residential care facilities for immobile residents to be taken outside for their regular dose of sunshine. This has been found to positively influence their mood.

Caution. Take precautions not to get sunburnt. Consider your climate and the time of year. Decide how long you are going to be out, and at what time of day, to safely get both your exercise and your dose of Vitamin D. Wear a hat and sunscreen.

Diet
There is a growing body of research looking into the link between the health of your gut and the health of your brain. Just think about how stress and anxiety impact on your digestive system and you will recognise that both how you eat and what you eat will have a significant impact on your emotional state. I have no intention of telling you exactly what to eat, but I would suggest you do some research yourself to see what healthy changes you can make to your diet that you can comfortably stick with.

What is important is balance and moderation. I'm not saying that you must give up your favourite comfort food. I am suggesting you look for ways to improve your way of eating by focusing on eating fewer unhealthy foods while building better food habits.

Common ideas about healthy ways of eating tend to focus on eating more:

- Fruit and vegetables
- Whole grains, legumes, nuts
- Fish and seafood
- Olive oil

Common ideas about healthy ways of eating tend to focus on eating less:

- Red and processed meats
- High-fat dairy products
- Saturated fats
- Highly refined carbohydrates and sugars

Please don't think I'm saying you should never eat a beef steak again. I'm not. Think balance and moderation. If the idea of changing your diet is confronting, then I would suggest starting the process of change gradually. You could choose, for example, to eat a smaller piece of steak and less potato, while adding more vegetables to the plate.

Stop and Smell the Roses
Stop and smell the roses is an old saying that will never lose its value. In fact, as the world becomes increasingly hectic, it is even more important that you take the time to stop and appreciate the simple things, whether it be the scent of a rose, a beautiful sunset, or the smell of the salt air as you walk on the beach.

Think about something simple that brings a sense of well-being, a sense of contentment to you, whether it is a hug from a loved one, hugging your dog or cat, singing along to your favourite song, doing a silly dance, or drinking a cup of tea or coffee. Walking barefoot on the grass, sitting under a tree, or feeling the sun on your face can help you take advantage of nature to improve your mood. There are no rules to say what simple thing will improve your mood in the moment. What is important is that you stop and take notice of those little things that make you feel good. When you feel good in the moment, you have successfully stepped away from the negative thoughts for a short time at least. More moments of feeling good equal fewer moments of depression.

Depression affects your motivation and your organisational skills. When you feel depressed you tend to do less and achieve less than when you are not feeling depressed. To combat depression and the inertia that attends it, it is important to set goals and make plans.

Setting Goals
Pre-planning prevents poor performance is an adage that will always ring true. The depression monster is brilliant at derailing your best intentions. To combat the enemy, you must have a plan and you must stick to that plan. To that end, it is important to not only have a plan but also to be aware of the pitfalls you may face. Your plan should include strategies to overcome the potential pitfalls.

One clever idea to help motivate you is to set yourself an initial goal that you are confident of achieving. Once you have achieved that victory it is easier to set and achieve your next goal. Success begets success. Victory begets further victories. This might be something as simple as choosing to have a Thai beef salad rather than battered fish and chips when you go out for lunch today. Another example might be choosing to walk the ten minutes to the café to buy your morning coffee rather than driving. Once you make a healthy choice, it's easier to make other healthy choices. The first step is the hardest, so make your first step as easy as possible.

Getting organised is vital when it comes to beating your old enemy, depression. One of the best ways to become more organised is to build more structure and routine into your life. Structure and routine take the guesswork out of your decisions. One significant impact of depression is a decline in your cognitive resources, which means effectively that your ability to think, plan and make decisions is less than normal. When you combine this with the lack of motivation that depression lays over you, it becomes very difficult to make good, clear decisions in the pressure of the moment. When you are depressed, even decisions such as what you are going to have for lunch can become difficult. There is a reason that many people when depressed tend to eat more junk food. The decision to prepare a healthy meal can just seem too hard in the heat of the moment. Much easier to simply ring and order a pizza with a side of garlic bread and a bottle of soft drink.

One way to get around the heat of the moment is to make plans and decisions before you need to carry them out. You can do this systematically and effectively through daily planning.

Daily Planning
Daily planning is a powerful and efficient way of setting and achieving your goals. Your daily plan is made the day before to take the pressure off you in the here and now. When you stop and think about what you can prepare for lunch tomorrow, it's much easier for you to make a healthy meal choice that can be relatively quick and easy to prepare. When lunchtime rolls around the following day you already know what you are having and how to prepare it. You are much more likely to follow through with a plan you have made previously as there's no pressure to make the decision in the moment.

The other advantage of planning meals ahead of time is that you will also organise to buy any ingredients you may need to create your gourmet masterpiece or simple salad before the time to prepare the meal rolls around. Imagine going to the kitchen to see what you could have for breakfast only to find there was no milk and no bread. For most people that would limit the choices considerably, and perhaps lead many people to skip breakfast altogether. When you plan your meals ahead of time that scenario simply won't happen.

Daily or pre-planning can be used to create regular routines as well as to increase your efficiency in achieving your goals. Initially you can use daily planning to build structure and routine into your day by sitting down the night before to create your plan for the following day. Depending on your needs, you can plan your entire day or simply plan your morning walk. There is no hard and fast rule. You may find starting by planning your morning walk and your meals works for you. Alternatively, you may take to the idea of setting goals for your whole day like a duck takes to water. It's entirely your choice.

When you are planning for tomorrow, there is a range of different areas that you might like to consider including in your plan:

- Exercise
- Diet
- Chores
- Work/study related activities
- Me time
- Social/family time
- Leisure activities
- Community activities

You might not set out to include all these areas in one day, but it's worthwhile remembering that all these areas are likely to be of relevance to you at some stage. You may even come up with ideas that I have not thought about including. Once again, your life, your plan, your rules.

I'll give a couple of examples of what incorporating daily planning might look like depending on how much routine and structure you choose.

Example A. Cathy works from home. She has been working on her daily planning for some time. She has put together a weekly template to increase her routine around the home. She has specific days in the week for different household chores such as washing, cleaning, and so on. Here I have outlined two days from Cathy's schedule.

Time	Monday	Tuesday
7am	Get up/put sheets on to wash	Get up/go for a walk
8am	Breakfast/hang sheets/dishes	Breakfast/put dishes in dishwasher
9am	Office work	Vacuum floors, clean toilet and bathroom
10am	Break/ring Mum	Office work
11am	Update tax records from last week	Post office and shopping
12pm	Lunch	Lunch
1pm	Relax with novel	Review and order stock
2pm	Pilates class	Office work
3pm	Coffee with girls from the class	Afternoon break
4pm	Check emails/orders	Check emails/orders
5pm	Plan schedule for tomorrow	Plan schedule for tomorrow
6pm	Prepare dinner	Prepare dinner

As you can see, building a routine and planning your daily activities can be an excellent mechanism for increasing the likelihood that you achieve your goals and optimising the way you spend your time.

Example B. Joe decides to start by focusing on exercise and diet. His first attempt on a day home looks like this:

Morning:	Get up when alarm goes off, get dressed and take the dog for a walk (40 minutes)
Once home:	Feed the dog then have a shower
	Breakfast – one egg on toast, black coffee, banana
Lunch:	Walk to the local café for lunch
	Chicken and salad wrap and a bottle of water
Dinner:	200g grilled rump steak with roasted broccoli, cauliflower and sweet potato

Joe is starting his journey by making some simple changes to his lifestyle choices, focusing on improving his diet and exercise level in a way that will have positive health benefits and serve to improve his emotional functioning. In other words, his level of depression will be lowered.

In her daily plan over the two days we sampled, Cathy has included items that fall into the areas of diet, exercise, social activities, work, chores, and me time. Both examples are realistic and both utilise the principal of prior planning.

Let's delve a little further into Cathy's story. Cathy lost her job ten months ago. She struggled with her mental health and was put on anti-depressants. She found her depression and social isolation growing and after a month or so started to see a psychologist. The psychologist encouraged her to increase her level of exercise, look at her diet, and discussed the concept of behavioural activation. The psychologist also introduced the idea of daily planning. Cathy started putting a daily plan together and found it helped her mood and organisational abilities. She subsequently planned and started up her new business. Six months down the track her business is going well, her fitness has improved, she has lost weight, and made new friends. She weaned off antidepressants two months ago and is feeling better in herself than she ever has.

Another strategy Cathy made good use of in her battle with depression was changing her way of thinking.

Addressing Negative Thoughts

It occurs to me that the depression monster tends to use the divide and conquer strategy quite effectively. "What on earth is she talking about now?" you might ask. Well, let me remind you of the metaphor I introduced in Chapter Five – the company of you with the boss and worker. Remember when you criticise yourself it is as though the boss is beating up on the worker. Your goal is to work towards becoming not just a good boss but building a truly respectful and appreciative culture within yourself. The health and success of your business very much depends on the good relationship you as the boss build with your worker. So be kind. Be appreciative. Be respectful of yourself. Don't listen to the depression monster who is trying hard to drive a wedge between your respective selves, and whatever you do, resist the temptation to do the monster's work for it. The bottom line here is to stop beating up on yourself. To do that you need to understand the nature of depressive thoughts.

Depressive thoughts are often about the past, beating up on yourself, telling yourself how useless you are, ruminating about all the stupid things you've done. You often predict your future by looking at all the failures of the past. When you allow yourself to buy into these thoughts, you can easily start to think of yourself as your own worst enemy.

Here's the thing, though – if you think of depression as the enemy, you realise that it is the depression monster whispering these terrible, soul-destroying thoughts into your mind's ear. When the thought appears in your mind you have a choice.

You can run with it, expand on it, and immerse yourself in the helplessness and hopelessness the monster is endeavouring to instil in you. If you take that route, the depression monster wins.

The alternative is to find a way of reframing the thought and/or letting the thought go. Reframing we covered in Chapter Four. Go back and review the chapter and remind yourself that you have simple and effective strategies to beat the sabotaging thoughts.

With depression, the most crippling sabotage you experience tends to come from your negative and self-limiting thoughts and the language you use to speak to yourself:

- All or nothing language

    - Stop telling yourself the situation is impossible. Shift your language to reflect that while the situation might be difficult it is possible to resolve it. It simply requires your commitment to not giving in, and the formation of a plan of attack. Be prepared to fight for yourself and your sense of well-being.

- Labelling

    - Remind yourself that calling yourself depressed is an old pattern. It does not have to be a current pattern.

- Blaming

    - Don't blame the monster. You can choose to take control of your own response.

- Pressure language

    - Stop creating chores for yourself. Instead, look at the likely outcome of doing the task and make a conscious choice as to whether it would be beneficial. If you decide it would not be beneficial, then scrap the idea. If you believe it would be beneficial or desirable, then plan to achieve that goal.

    - Choose to move and then keep moving forward away from inertia and stagnation. Move away from the depression monster!

The Swamp Monster

An alternative to reframing your thoughts is to use mindfulness strategies to let go of your negative and self-limiting thoughts. Even a simple mindfulness of breathing exercise can serve to distract you from the negative thoughts. When you notice the negative thought, simply:

- Take a deep breath into your eyes.
- Continue to breathe deeply, focusing your attention on your breath. Notice the sensation of the breath.
- If a thought intrudes, simply notice the thought, then let it go and return your attention to your breath.
- Repeat as necessary.

This is a very simple strategy that works by both shifting you into relax mode through the breathing exercise and distracting you from your thoughts by getting you to shift your focus from your thought back to your breath.

If you want to get creative with mindfulness strategies for letting go of thoughts you can search online and find a strategy that appeals to you. One example that I hear used frequently is to use your senses to notice three things you can see, three things you can hear, three things you can touch, and so on.

Alternatively, you could imagine your thoughts as ripples in the water, leaves floating down a stream, birds landing in a tree then flying away again, fluffy clouds floating by in a blue sky, or cars driving down the road. Anything that comes and goes could be used as an example. I'm sure you can come up with your own analogies here. Personally, I prefer to imagine nature than traffic, but each to their own.

Let your thoughts turn up, float through, and then disappear.

When you think about it, you have thoughts popping in and out of your mind all the time. Your mind is a veritable chatterbox. Think about the many times you have been listening to someone or even watching television and your mind has wandered off on a tangent. You might start thinking about what you're doing for dinner tonight, your upcoming holiday, or something that happened last week. It doesn't really matter what it is. What is important is that as soon as you realise you are missing what's being said, you let go of the interrupting thought and return your attention to the person or program you were listening to. I am certain this has happened to you.

The point I'm making here is that you frequently and easily let go of your intrusive thoughts and redirect your attention somewhere else. There is no difference between a positive thought, neutral thought, or negative thought in this case. A thought is a thought is a thought. If you can let go of a thought that has distracted you from what you were doing and return your attention to where you feel it should be, then you can let go of a negative thought and direct your attention somewhere else. It's the same principle.

A thought only has the power you choose to give it. So, if a thought is not helpful, limit its power by choosing to let go of it.

IN SUMMARY

Depression is an enemy you can fight. Think of it as an enemy rather than part of you and you can find the determination and courage to beat it. All you need do is make a plan and follow through. There are some relatively simple changes you can make that will serve you well in your battle. Some simple lifestyle changes are known to have a positive impact on your mood and overall sense of wellbeing, such as:

- a healthy diet
- regular exercise
- sunshine – spend time outdoors
- mindfulness – stop and smell the roses

Some positive changes you can make to your behaviour and thought patterns to beat depression include:

- behavioural activation – start moving to keep moving
- daily planning – pre-planning prevents poor performance and allows you to achieve your goals
- practise letting go of, or reframing, negative thoughts

The strategies you can use to beat depression are not difficult to understand. It is also easier to fight when you know who you are and the nature of the enemy you are fighting. Because of the sneaky way depression has of sapping your energy, it takes effort to start fighting, but once you start it becomes easier to keep building your momentum.

The first step is to make the effort and start moving. The first step is the hardest but is so worth the effort. You can do this. You can fight the battle with the depression monster. You can win! Trust in yourself. You've got this!

CHAPTER TEN

Breaking the Big Bad Wolf of Habits

I spoke about breaking habits in Chapter Three. The information in that chapter likely helped you shift away from some of the habits that simply were not working for you. Most habits are relatively simple to change when you identify the habit you want to break, recognise that the habit can be broken or changed, and make a plan as to what you will do instead of the old habit. Then it's simply a matter of practising the new behaviour until it, in turn, becomes habit.

What I didn't do in that chapter, however, is consider how to change habits that may be more resistant to change. Habits can be resistant to change for various reasons. You may have a habit that you want to change but that you nonetheless get some pleasure from. I'm thinking about cigarettes or alcohol as I write this, but it may be something as simple as biting your nails.

I am not an expert in addiction, and I am not intending to offer a guide to dealing with addiction. What I will do in this chapter is to give you a plan of attack for beating habits that have in the past been resistant to change.

Habits that are resistant to change tend to stay with you for a variety of reasons, including:

- They are rewarding.
- They are associated with other things you enjoy.
- They are triggered by emotional distress.
- Multiple diverse triggers are associated with the habit.
- You have always thought of the habit simply as part of who you are.
- You have never realised you can change the habit.
- You have not prepared yourself properly to break the habit.
- You have never been truly committed to breaking the habit.

While I am not going to talk about addictions per se, I will briefly mention the Stages of Change Model which was originally introduced in the late 1970s by researchers, James

Prochaska and Carlo DiClemente. I will consider a five-stage model often used by experts working with addiction:

1. Precontemplation: you do not feel your habit is problematic and you are not planning to change.
2. Contemplation: you are beginning to see your habit as a problem, but you have mixed feelings about it. Your habit has its good and bad points.
3. Preparation: You recognise your habit is problematic. The bad points outweigh the good points. You may have already tried changing the habit in the recent past, or you are preparing to make change.
4. Action: You are actively involved in changing your habit and feel you are making progress. You may still be struggling with the change and are at risk of relapse if the temptation overwhelms you or you become emotionally reactive.
5. Maintenance: You can avoid any temptations to return to the habit. You have learned to deal with temptations to use the habit, and you have successfully developed more adaptive behaviours to replace the old habit. If you slip into the old habit, you are able to reset and not see this as failure.

I think this model gives some helpful clues as to what is necessary for you to change an entrenched habit that has pros and cons attached to it. If you are weighing up the costs and benefits of a habit, it's likely to be more difficult to change than if you can clearly see a habit is unhelpful.

Let's use smoking cigarettes as an example of a complex and hard to break habit. Smoking cigarettes can be a difficult habit to break because your reasons for smoking tend to be multi-faceted. For example:

- You may be addicted to the nicotine, which means your body craves the hit of nicotine.
    - Note that not everyone that smokes cigarettes is addicted to nicotine.
    - One clue that you might be addicted to nicotine is that your breakfast consists of a cigarette (often with coffee). Of course, you may not be addicted to nicotine and still have a cigarette for breakfast.
- Smoking is a habit you have chosen for yourself at some stage in your life.
- You may smoke because you think it improves your image.
- You may smoke partly due to peer pressure.
- You may particularly enjoy some of the cigarettes you smoke in the day, for example, you may enjoy a cigarette at the end of a meal.
- You may link smoking with drinking.
- Smoking can be a social activity
    - with friends who also smoke.
    - acting as a connection with other people you don't know but with whom you're sharing a smoking space.

Breaking the Big Bad Wolf of Habits

- Certain people in your life may act as a trigger for you to smoke.
- You may use smoking cigarettes as a stress relief strategy.
- You may see smoking cigarettes as relaxing.
- Having a cigarette may provide an excuse to have a well-deserved break from work.
- You may believe that you think better while smoking a cigarette.
- You may smoke when you're bored.
- You may smoke because you believe it will suppress your appetite and help you lose weight.
- You may believe that smoking is a difficult habit to break.
- You may have tried quitting before and failed.
- You may believe that you do not have the willpower to give up smoking.
- You may believe that being a smoker is part of who you are. It's your self-identity.
- You can't imagine yourself as a non-smoker.
- You may have cut down the number of cigarettes you smoke but struggle to stop completely because you are ambivalent about the idea of never having another cigarette.
- You may have a view of reformed smokers as being completely intolerant and unreasonable.
- Any other reasons that you can think of . . .

If you are a smoker reading through this list, you are no doubt nodding along to a number of these reasons. If you want to give up smoking make a list of the reasons that make quitting so hard for you.

If you are a non-smoker but have a different habit of your own that has proven resistant to change, compile your own list of reasons to explain to yourself why breaking your habit is so difficult.

The idea behind identifying the reasons you engage in the habit, and struggle to change it, is to allow you to get to know the enemy. The better you know your enemy, the better your plan of attack will be. Knowledge is power. Knowledge of why your habit is so tricky to break will provide you with the very clues you need to successfully break it. Your goal is to devise a successful plan to allow you to step away from your complex habit. In a case like this the plan is not necessarily going to be a single solution that fits all circumstances.

Smoking is a perfect example. There is a big difference between a cigarette you have when you are having a beer with John and he lights up, and the cigarette you have when you are trying to control the stress you feel before going into that incredibly important job interview.

Yes, there's more to it than you likely realised . . . and yes, that's why giving up smoking can be so very difficult. As I've said in other chapters, however, pre-planning prevents poor performance. Pre-planning also provides solutions.

Breaking the Big Bad Wolf of Habits

In order to successfully break any habit you must have some understanding of why the habit exists and what function it serves. In a complex case like smoking, there will be a variety of functions to be considered. In essence, that means that you may also need a variety of alternative strategies to replace the behaviour in different circumstances.

Let's consider my version of the Stages of Change as they relate to resistant habits, such as smoking.

1. In the precontemplation stage you are not considering changing your habit. Other people might be pointing out that you have a problem, but realistically you are not going to change your behaviour until you see your behaviour as an issue. Change cannot be forced on you, and unless you're prepared to step up and take responsibility for making changes yourself it just won't happen, so let's skip over this stage.

2. In the contemplation stage, you are starting to suspect that perhaps you do have a problem with this particular habit, but you can also see the benefits in the habit. You may start to think about making small changes to your habit, but commitment to real change is unlikely.

3. In the preparation stage, I suggest that you:

    a. set a goal for yourself in terms of the date by which you are going to be rid of your resistant habit, for example, I will be a non-smoker by the time I get to my birthday in three months' time. On my birthday I will be a non-smoker. Tell yourself this regularly to prime yourself for the change. Visualise waking up and not wanting a cigarette. Visualise what it will be like when you have left the old habit behind and embraced better habits in its place. This visualisation technique will help get your unconscious system (the worker) on-board with your plans and preparing for the change.

b. research your habit and spend some time recording instances of the habit and what led to each instance. In other words, what were the circumstances surrounding the instance, what was your emotional state, what do you think was your motivation in that particular instance? Record this information in a table format for a week, or as long as necessary to identify your behavioural patterns. This will give you some useful data around your habit. You should by then be able to identify the main influences that affect your habit, for example, stress, habit, boredom, peer pressure.

The preparation stage is essential if you are going to get the knowledge to fight the habit and win. Doing the research gives you the information you will use to break the old habit while allowing you to devise new, effective patterns of behaviour that will serve you better than the old habit. You know the new behaviours will work because you know exactly what your motivation was for each situation you studied in this stage. Knowledge is power. Pre-planning prevents poor performance and therefore is essential for success.

The preparation stage is also essential for priming your entire system – the subconscious system (the worker) and the conscious system (the boss) – with an expectation of success. You are visualising yourself after you have succeeded in changing the habit. You are setting up a prophecy of your future and you are then going on to do the work necessary to make it happen. The unconscious system will work on preparing your body for change. The conscious system will integrate the information you gather and create the plans around changing the old habit.

4. The action stage comes after you have done the groundwork and you know exactly why you fall into the trap of trotting out the habit in various circumstances. At this point you can make a solid plan to counter each reason the habit rears its head. This might mean developing a number of different plans that deal with:

   a. your emotional reactions to different circumstances, such as stress or boredom.

   b. the habit itself, for example, "I always have a cigarette after dinner".

   c. physical situations that influence you to engage in the habit, such as hanging out with the smokers at a party.

The action stage involves the process of putting the plan in place, tweaking it as necessary, and practising the new patterns as they become easier. You will likely have some slips along the way to the next phase, but you have the knowledge, skills, and perseverance to succeed.

Remember, it is human to slip. No human is perfect. You have a good understanding by now of exactly who you are, and having practised the tools I gave you in the first two sections of this book, I hope you recognise how awesome you are. You can achieve any realistic goal you set for yourself with knowledge of yourself (tick) and knowledge of what the goal entails (tick).

From here on, it's simply a matter of practice and consolidation of the strategies you have developed through research of the habit and knowledge of yourself.

5. The final stage is maintenance. By now, your new operations manual is in place and every part of you knows the new patterns of behaviour that are turning quickly into useful and effective habits. You can cope easily with difficult scenarios. You have reached your goal of breaking that complex and nasty old habit. You are awesome. Pat yourself on the back and keep moving along the path that you have deliberately chosen for yourself.

Let's work through an example and see what this system might look like in practice.

Case Study A – Quit Smoking

Dave is a 50-year-old male who has been smoking cigarettes for 35 years. His doctor has recently diagnosed him with Chronic Obstructive Pulmonary Disease (COPD) and has told him to quit smoking for his health. He has a sedentary but stressful job. He has a family history of heart disease, and his doctor has told him he is at increased risk of a heart attack or a stroke, as well as an escalation of his COPD. Dave has a nine-year-old son and has realised if he doesn't change his habits, he may not be around to see him grow up. Dave is ready to give up smoking but is concerned about his ability to do so as he tried and failed to give up 12 months ago.

Dave saw a psychologist in February who encouraged him to set the date by which time he would be a non-smoker. He decided to be a non-smoker by his son's tenth birthday on the fifth of May.

He was then asked to collect some data on his smoking habit. The table below gives a single day snapshot of Dave's habit.

WED 26 FEB

Time	Cigs	Why
7am	2	B'fast
8am	1	Drive - Work
9am	2	Stress
12pm	2	Lunch
2pm	2	Break
5pm	3	Pub with S.
6pm	1	Drive - Home
8-10pm	3	Relaxing
	16	

As Dave collected the data for the first week, he noted that he tends to smoke more when he is not in the office, and that his smoking intake goes up when he is feeling stressed or under pressure. He identified a few people both from work and his social circle that he tends to smoke around.

Dave noted that his wife does not smoke and that he doesn't smoke inside their house. He does smoke in his car, however. He said that this particular Wednesday was probably a fairly typical workday in terms of his cigarette smoking.

When Dave presented his findings, he and the psychologist identified several different triggers for his smoking:

- Possible addiction to nicotine. Dave regularly starts his day with a cigarette and coffee for breakfast. He noticed that his craving for a cigarette would get stronger at regular intervals. If he was able to have a cigarette at that time he would. If it was not possible to have a cigarette, the craving would eventually go away. His psychologist explained that nicotine cravings would come in a slow wave-like pattern, ebbing and flowing. She noted that if he could ride the wave without a cigarette the craving would probably subside on its own.

- Habit. This included the cigarettes when relaxing, driving by himself, or at the pub.

- Stress. Dave would smoke before and after stressful meetings.

- Influence of other smokers. Dave noted a tendency to smoke when other people smoke.

Dave decided on a graduated approach to giving up smoking as he had a little over two months in which to reach his goal of being a non-smoker. The first cigarettes he decided to target were the stress-related cigarettes. Dave began to notice and reframe his negative language. Over the next two weeks, Dave used several strategies to better manage his work stress:

- He started walking on a more regular basis, choosing to go for a brisk 20-minute walk at lunch time instead of sitting with his smoker friends.

- To further calm his body and mind, Dave also started practising the breathing through his eyes technique which allowed him to both relax in a stressful situation and think more clearly under pressure.

- He continued to note his tendency to self-sabotage through his thoughts when he was stressed. He became more efficient at reframing his negative thoughts.

- He began to prioritise his work tasks more efficiently by regularly reviewing his outstanding tasks and considering their relative importance and urgency. As a result, he found that his problem-solving abilities and his time management in the workplace improved.

- Dave started keeping water on his desk to regularly hydrate through the day. He found that stopping and taking a few slow sips of water helped him calm down and ground himself when the pressures of the job escalated. Also, he came to realise that sipping water was often enough to see him through the peak of each wave of nicotine craving when it came around.

With these strategies in place, Dave found that over the course of two weeks he was able to eliminate most of the cigarettes he was smoking at work. He still had the occasional cigarette break with his colleagues, but he deliberately chose not to smoke because he was feeling stressed. His sense of self-control grew and he realised he was feeling much more confident that he could eliminate cigarettes from his life entirely.

Within four weeks, Dave was down to a maximum of five cigarettes a day. He was still smoking two cigarettes first thing in the morning and smoking up to three cigarettes in the afternoon and evening. Dave reviewed his reasons for smoking each of these cigarettes.

Through this process, he recognised he was no longer craving cigarettes when stressed or distracted by activities even outside of work. Consequently, he wasn't going to the pub with Steve after work as often because he rarely felt the need to debrief. As an added bonus, Dave realised he was spending more quality time with his family because he was getting home earlier. It gave him more time to play with his son before dinner.

Dave realised he was still smoking when he got together with his mates, but nowhere near the same number of cigarettes as previously. He realised that these cigarettes were simply habit cigarettes. He was in the habit of smoking and drinking with this social set. Dave realised he would have to make a plan in order to eliminate social smoking. Considering his options, he realised he could stop getting together with his mates when they were likely to smoke, or he could plan not to smoke when he was in their company.

Dave decided he would continue to catch up with his mates and not smoke. He planned a strategy to make this possible:

- He would make sure he stood out of the line of the cigarette smoke as much as possible as that might act as a trigger.

  On a side note, as he was reducing his intake of cigarettes, Dave was noticing that the smell of cigarettes seemed stronger and not as appealing as it used to be. This was likely his unconscious system at work prepping his body and senses to not find the physical act of smoking appealing.

- He would limit how much alcohol he drank with his friends. He would limit himself to two alcoholic drinks so that his willpower to not smoke stayed strong. Over the previous month, Dave had noticed that after more than two drinks he tended to smoke more cigarettes than normal.

These changes worked well for Dave. He noticed that he was losing weight and feeling healthier with the changes that he had made at work and in social settings. Dave decided to bite the proverbial bullet and give up the final few cigarettes he was smoking. He decided to make his car a non-smoking zone. He cleaned his car and spent time getting rid of the tobacco smell that always seemed to be there. He decided he would distract himself in the car by listening to music. He compiled a library of songs to listen to that he knew he would enjoy. Dave found that when he started listening to music in the car, the drive to and from work became less stressful. He realised he wasn't missing the cigarettes and the stale tobacco smell in the car.

Two weeks out from his son's birthday, Dave lit up a cigarette and realised he wasn't enjoying the taste at all. He looked at the cigarette, took another drag, then put it out. He realised he no longer had the desire to smoke. Dave's subconscious system had done a good job of eliminating his physical enjoyment of cigarettes. His last few cigarettes each day had been smoked purely from habit. He recognised that he hadn't been enjoying them for some time.

Dave's son had his tenth birthday and Dave was there with him to enjoy it.

Dave is now a non-smoker. He is also fitter, stronger, healthier, and his COPD symptoms have decreased somewhat as his health and fitness have improved. Dave has confidence in himself that he can continue to develop healthier habits. He has continued to work to reduce his old tendency to sabotage himself with his thoughts and is feeling much more resilient. He reported feeling much better about himself in general. He noted that the changes he has put in place have impacted also on his relationships. His family life is much more relaxed, and he said that he and his wife are communicating better than ever. His son seems to enjoy his company much more and they are doing more father/son activities than previously. At work, Dave feels he is getting more respect from his colleagues and his bosses, and he feels that his work has improved as he is managing his stressors more effectively. "All in all," Dave said, "life is good."

Dave has achieved his goal of becoming a non-smoker and in so doing has developed a range of more adaptive habits and behaviours that are having a flow-on effect in his life. Dave is learning to be content within himself.

Case Study B – Anger Management

Ross is a 28-year-old male who identified as having anger management issues. He said on interview that he had always had a short fuse and as a child threw massive temper tantrums when he didn't get his own way. He said his dad also had a short fuse and yelled a lot while his mum tried to be the peacemaker in the family. Ross and his wife have a three-year-old daughter and have just had a baby boy.

Ross is a qualified carpenter working with a firm of builders. He reported that his work has been suffering of late because of his tendency to fly into a rage when something goes wrong. He said lots of things seem to have been going wrong lately. Ross noted that a year ago he was given quite a lot of responsibility at work, training apprentices and running a job when the boss was absent. Recently, he said, he feels lucky they haven't sacked him. He said that he cost the company a fair bit of money on the last job when he messed up and caused some damage after losing his temper.

On the home front, Ross was distressed to report that his little daughter seemed to be frightened of him, hiding behind her mother when he came into the room. He said she would hardly talk to him these days. His wife has tried to be understanding of his stress, but when the new baby was born, she told him in no uncertain terms that he had to see someone about his anger. She has threatened to leave him and go to her parents with the children if he doesn't sort himself out.

Recognising that his life was in danger of falling apart if he didn't do something about his anger, Ross went to see a psychologist.

The psychologist went through the strategies I have given you in Section One of this book. She taught him about the autonomic nervous system, about the thinking brain which is responsible for proactive behaviour versus the reactive loop which leads him to react like a three-year-old. She taught him to breathe through his eyes to help him relax and create the space he would need to pull back from his reactive behaviour. Ross learned to recognise his potential to sabotage himself through his negative language and thoughts and learned how to reframe his language.

In spite of being proactive in putting the strategies into play, Ross still found he was struggling with his temper. He was able to use the strategies to stop his anger exploding but commented that he was still getting angry very quickly just as he always has. He shrugged his shoulders and said, "That's just me. I've always been like that."

The psychologist pointed out that he was continuing to fall into the trap of labelling himself and his behaviour. He was continuing to buy into his self-limiting beliefs. She asked him why he believed that the anger was part of him. He replied that he got it from his dad and people had always commented on his hair-trigger temper.

Breaking the Big Bad Wolf of Habits

In the conversation that followed, the psychologist suggested to Ross that his angry outbursts were a habit like any other. She encouraged Ross to consider the possible explanations for his long-term anger management issues. How did he come to develop the habit in the first place, and why did he then maintain the habit? Ross identified the following issues:

- My dad modelled the same behaviour.
- I was always told I had a temper.
- I was frequently rewarded for my tantrums by getting my own way.
- The other boys thought I was tough. "I think they were scared of my temper."
- I never realised I didn't have to have anger management issues.

The psychologist pointed out that everyone takes on stories about who they are and their place in the world by the time they are about seven or eight years of age.

These stories sit in the core of you, in your gut if you like, and you rarely question them. You do not create these stories yourself. They develop through your experiences as a kid. They are strongly influenced by your parents, the examples they set, how they treat you. They are also influenced by interactions with other people when you are very young. They can be influenced by your experiences as a child. These stories become your self-limiting beliefs and you tend to simply accept them as truth.

Ross took on the story that he couldn't control his temper and it had never occurred to him to question that self-limiting belief until now. It was a revelation. He recognised that over the past couple of weeks of therapy, while he had still felt himself get angry, he had actually been able to control his temper very quickly using the strategies he had been given.

The psychologist pointed out that his ability to quickly step away from the anger was more important than his initial angry reaction. Everyone feels reactive at times but not everyone acts on that reactive impulse. It's the ability to take control of your behaviour and choose your response that counts. If you focus on your proactive response instead of focusing on the initial annoyance, you can ditch the label and quickly change your habit.

She went on to say that while he kept labelling himself as having anger management issues he was perpetuating that self-limiting belief and perpetuating the habit. The problem with labelling is that it focuses your attention on the old habit and denies your ability to change. So even if you are pulling back from the anger each time it rears its head, if you keep telling yourself you are an angry young man, you will continue to be an angry young man. The habit will be maintained, and it will continue to be hard work for you to stop falling into the temper tantrum trap.

If, however, you tell yourself the anger is an old pattern of behaviour and that you now have a better way of responding when things don't go your way, then the new strategies will start to become your new habits. When that happens the old habit of lashing out will simply disappear.

Four weeks later, Ross reported that he was no longer feeling like an angry young man. He reported that he was much more relaxed and feeling good about himself. He felt far less stressed, and his attention at work was much better. He reported that things at home had improved out of sight. He and his wife were getting on better than they ever had, and his daughter was excited to see him when he came home. Work also was going well, and the boss had pulled him aside a week ago and commented on how much he had changed, how much his work had improved, and what a good influence he was becoming for the younger guys.

Three months after that, Ross had his last session with the psychologist. He told her that in the previous month, he had only had one episode where he chose to get up and walk away from a situation. He went outside for a few minutes while he breathed through his eyes and decided on the best course of action. He said before starting therapy he was angry every single day, and in a situation like that he would just have exploded. He now realises how much better he feels not feeling angry all the time. "For the first time in my life I feel in control. It's great."

IN SUMMARY

Habits can be resistant to change for various reasons. What's important when tackling any Big Bad Wolf of a Habit is to go through the following steps systematically:

1. Be thorough in investigating and understanding why the habit is so difficult to shift, what situations trigger the habit, and what your beliefs are about the habit. This is the information gathering stage that provides knowledge. As you know, knowledge is power!

2. When planning your strategies to change the habit, it is important to review the information you have gathered and decide whether each presentation of the habit can be dealt with in the same way, or whether different presentations will require different strategies to change it. For example, smoking because you feel stressed is a different presentation to smoking with your mates in the pub. The strategic plan you put together to stop your habit of smoking when stressed is not likely to be effective in stopping you smoking in a social setting with other smokers. Different presentations require different plans and strategies.

3. When planning to change a habit you have previously enjoyed and that you very much see as a fundamental part of you, it is important to plan ahead and set yourself a specific time frame for

achieving your goal. Give yourself time to adapt and accept the change, for example, I will be a non-smoker by my birthday in two months' time. Telling yourself you will stop smoking tomorrow is unlikely to work for most of you. You need time for your conscious and unconscious systems to take on the new idea and adapt to it.

4. Start by setting readily achievable goals on your journey to change the unwanted habit. Success begets success. Success begets belief in yourself. Once you have a victory under your belt it's easier to work up to more demanding challenges. Start with the easy to change aspects of the habit and work up to the more difficult aspects when setting your goals.

5. Utilise the strategies you already have in place to help you change other unwanted habits.

- Breathe through your eyes to relax your system and help you think better
- Reframe or let go of negative thoughts
- Ground yourself in moments of distress
- Use mindfulness strategies to reset to the present moment
- Gather information about the situation you are facing
- Plan and problem-solve

About the Author

Dr Tracey Zielinski is an experienced clinical psychologist who has run her own private practice since 2011. She has worked as a clinical psychologist and neuropsychologist in both public and private settings for over 20 years. Tracey obtained her PhD from the University of Queensland in 2006.

Over the years, Tracey has developed her own education-based therapeutic process which she says can best be described as common-sense psychology. Through this process, her adult clients have learned to increase their resilience to cope with a range of emotional and personal challenges including stress, anxiety, adjustment disorders, depression, anger management, trauma, and chronic health conditions. The process is generally based on principles of cognitive behaviour therapy and mindfulness.

With the rise of the COVID-19 global pandemic Tracey started to reflect on the mental health crisis highlighted by the impact of the virus, enforced lockdowns, grief and loss, financial stresses, and the social isolation many people around the world are facing. Mental health professionals are being overwhelmed by the public demand.

The global pandemic has highlighted the need for new and effective ways of helping people back to a sense of security and control in their lives. Recognising the ever-increasing demands we of the human race face living in this complex world, Tracey has chosen to write *Get it Together Forever* to share the simplicity of her process with a wider audience than she can hope to see for individual therapy. The idea behind the book is not to provide therapy for people with serious mental health concerns, but rather to reach out to those people who are able to independently step into control of their own actions and reactions when given the knowledge and strategies to do so.

Tracey was born and raised in Queensland, Australia, and continues to call Queensland her home. She and her husband are enthusiastic supporters of theatre, music, and the arts. Tracey dabbles in a range of creative activities, playing a little music, making up silly little ditties to encourage her husband in his eye-rolling, acting in community theatre productions, and creating clever little metaphors to add to her therapeutic arsenal. She hopes one day to put her writing skills to a different purpose and write her first novel.

For more information:

Website: www.getittogetherforever.com

Email: drtraceyzielinski@gmail.com

Acknowledgements

I would like to acknowledge the following people for their contributions to this book over the years:

My brother, who introduced me to the idea of breathing through my eyes.

Judith Richards, who helped me step away from my self-limiting beliefs.

Natasa and Stuart Denman and their amazing Ultimate 48 Hour Author team, without whom this book would still be in the planning stage.

Notes

Get it Together Forever

Notes

Get it Together Forever

Notes

www.ingramcontent.com/pod-product-compliance
Lightning Source LLC
Chambersburg PA
CBHW021832110526
R18278200001B/R182782PG44588CBX00004B/3